# REJECTED

## The Story of an African American Man in Search of Himself

## DES A. PENNINGTON

*Published by* So It Is Written, LLC
Rochester, MI
**SoItIsWritten.net**

*Rejected: The Story of an African American Man in Search of Himself*
Copyright © 2025 by Des A. Pennington

*Edited by:* So It Is Written – www.SoItIsWritten.net

*Formatting:* Ya Ya Ya Creative – YaYaYaCreative@gmail.com

ISBN: 979-8-9912588-9-0

LCCN: 2025909673

PRINTED AND BOUND IN THE UNITED STATES OF AMERICA

# Table of Contents

# The Early Years

## Memories

*"It takes a moment to make memories
and a lifetime to forget them."*
—ANDY MINEO

S leeping comfortably on the floor next to Momma—who was lying on a pallet of blankets—I was suddenly awakened by the sound of her moaning. I was overcome with an awkward feeling of helplessness. Suddenly, a few grownups came from somewhere in the house—one grabbing the kid that was lying on her chest, taking him somewhere else—and the other kneeling down on the floor between her legs, telling Momma to push. After some time, I heard a baby's cry. Then, sirens, followed by more people coming into the room.

While those people placed Momma and the baby on a stretcher, taking them away, I vividly remember thinking, *What about me?* They never even acknowledged the existence of the child sitting on the discarded blankets right next to her.

I now realize that the first memory of my existence was the birth of one of my younger brothers, either Jamel (b. 12/29/1970) or Dwight (b. 2/17/1972). Studies have shown that the earliest memories people recall point to when they were two-and-a-half, which, in my case, makes sense since I must have been as young as two or as old as four years of age during this time.

I was born on December 27, 1968. I'm the fourth of the six children birthed by Loretta Wadley, who became a Pennington after marrying her on-again, off-again boyfriend, Joseph Benjamin Pennington. Rosa Wadley (b. 9/17/1963), Joseph Benjamin, II (b. 11/09/1966), and Petris Georval (b. 2/07/1967) were my older siblings from that union. Shortly after I was born, Momma divorced. She later gave birth to my two younger brothers, Jamel Donlue Moore and Dwight DeAngelo Howard Moore—both of whom were fathered by a long-time family friend who Momma and her siblings grew up with: Desmond Moore. Though we had different fathers, all of our last names are Pennington because Momma wanted it that way.

The spotted memories of my toddler years seemed somber, though filled with lots of laughter. I was always surrounded by my siblings, piled up in one room in the dark. Yet, I strangely felt secure—right up until that security was taken away for the first time.

As usual, my siblings and I were in one room, lying on our pallet on the floor. Yet, this time, the baby was crying uncontrollably. My sister and older siblings were frantically feeling around the floor, trying to search for his bottle to comfort him. Still, for some reason, it was nowhere to be found. It was then that I first noticed that Momma was seldom on the pallet with us in the dark—and, more importantly, that the darkness was due to the lights not working.

My brother Petris, whom we call "Pat," began lighting the matches he had in his hand, which had apparently been given to him to use as a light during the night. Pat lit some papers and walked out of the room on a mission to find a bottle to feed the baby. After a short time, he returned with a fresh bottle and laid down with us as my sister, Rosa, fed the baby to keep him quiet.

Sometime after, I was awakened by the smell of smoke. Soon, my sister yelled, "Fire!" Either Pat or our oldest brother, Joe, opened the door of the room and quickly closed it. All we could see were the bright colors of the flames that had taken over everything beyond the room we were in. I don't know where they got the instincts, but one of them stuffed blankets around the bottom of the door to prevent smoke from getting through. At the same time, the other motioned for us to cuddle near the window of the room. There we sat, cuddled around each other with a blanket over our heads, scared out of our wits while coughing and crying for Momma. Then, just before we became overwhelmed with the smoke coming from the blazing fire, somebody burst through the window of the room, taking us out one by one—beginning with my sister Rosa handing him the baby. One of the neighbors had become aware of the fire and rushed into action to save us before fire trucks even arrived.

Then the questions began: "Where's your parents?"

"Are you here alone?"

"Are they in there by themselves?"

Once it was determined that we were indeed in the house all by ourselves, I felt ashamed by the looks of disgust and some woman shouting, "Their Momma ain't never home! She always leaves them by themselves at night!"

# Separation

I took my first car ride the evening of the fire after what seemed like hours of people standing around, seemingly discussing what they were going to do with us. I overheard multiple people asking if anyone had been able to contact our mother. After a while, though I could see Momma talking to people, some total strangers put a few of my siblings and me in the back of their car and drove away.

We were calling out for Momma, but the people wouldn't let us talk to her. For the entire ride, I held both the baby and my other little brother close to me to keep us warm since the inside of the car was cold. When we finally stopped, we were taken to a place that smelled clean, yet it was cold. I had no idea where we were. All I knew was I wanted Momma and my other siblings. A woman came into the room we were waiting in, took both of my younger brothers, and later came to get me after what seemed like hours. She led me to what I thought was the place they had taken my siblings.

Much to my surprise, once again, I was alone—though there were other kids in the room I didn't know. For some reason, the chill and the smell of the unfamiliar air for the first time brought this eerie feeling of loneliness I had never experienced before. As I struggled to make sense of my surroundings, I saw things moving in the darkened room as I lay all by myself in a bunk bed, weeping. I wept from fright because, not only did I see shadows moving throughout the room, but I also distinctly recall hearing drops of water, people talking in the distance, and the sounds of the sniffles of others in the room—obviously weeping as they lay in their own strange place. It was then that I realized my siblings and I not only used each other for warmth while lying on our pallet on the floor but also as a reassurance to one another that we would be okay as long as we had each other.

Roger de Bussy-Rabutin once said, "Absence is to love what wind is to fire; it extinguishes the small, it inflames the great." I had never been so afraid in my life. Not even the fire made me feel fear like this because we were together during the fire. Once again, all I could think about was why they would separate me from my siblings and, more importantly, why I was all alone. For me, being alone comes with a peculiar smell—an uncomfortable fear that I can't explain to this day and a certain coldness that seems to outweigh anything else. For this reason, I've spent my life making sure I would never be alone.

Don't get me wrong, I enjoy being by myself sometimes; yet, I've come to realize that there is a difference between being by yourself and being alone. It took years for me to understand that I was actually an introverted extrovert because I loved being by myself and I loved being alone in my thoughts, as long as there were other people around. For this reason, I have made many choices I now consider questionable in an effort to simply surround myself with anybody just to keep that feeling of loneliness away!

Once a week, I went to a room with seats and toys. One by one, my siblings were brought into the room where we'd all get a chance to see Momma and play together for some time. But one day, Momma finally got to take us all home!

# Home

Our first home was actually a basement apartment on Clairmont Street in Detroit. As I sit here typing, I'm amazed that I actually remember the name of the street because I was much too young to read at the time. Yet, I have always remembered where that apartment was and the fun adventures we had there as a family.

People sat outside the apartment all the time, laughing and talking while the neighborhood children played. One of the parents would give us kids a quarter or a nickel, and we'd all make our way down the street to the store. We came back with brown paper bags filled with candy. Sometimes, we'd have so much change that one of us would have to go back another day to spend it all.

Let's just say that life back then seemed great! Even when we had to stay in the house because Momma wasn't home, we always found a game we could play. One of the indoor games was called War, where the little toy soldiers we had were lined up on either side of the room. We used rubber bands to shoot at the opponent's side until all the toy soldiers were knocked down. We also played hide-and-seek, wrestled with each other, or raced from wall to wall to see who was the fastest. The best game was when we looked out the window shades to watch people's feet as they walked by our basement apartment.

One day, Momma told us that we had to go outside all day because the landlord had placed a notice on the door that he was "dropping a bomb" in the apartment. While I had no idea what a bomb was, we were all excited simply to be outside all day. When we finally were allowed to go back into the apartment, I was overwhelmed by two things:

1. The pungent odor that could only be described as wet dirt smothered in pepper and

2. The sight of thousands of dead roaches that seemed to cover the entire floor

Momma was so disgusted by the number of bugs she had to clean up. She made it known to anybody who could hear as she screamed at the landlord at the top of her lungs about how nasty it was.

I had never heard Momma raise her voice at anybody. So, the very sight of it both scared me *and* made me proud that Momma was our protector. The crazy thing is I always saw roaches in the apartment—I had just never seen so many all at once! Sometime later, another one of those notes was put on the door; yet this time, Momma refused to let them in with the bomb on the appointed date. Momma had apparently decided she was out of the roach clean-up business.

Shortly thereafter, we moved to the upstairs side of a two-family flat on a street called Quincey. Quincey is the home where I began to "become." Though I was no more than four years old when we moved there, it was there that I started to truly be aware of everything that surrounded me. The living room had a huge picture window that faced a major street (Grand River) where I'd stand, lost in my mind, watching the movement of the many cars, buses, and people going from place to place. I spent hours daydreaming of the possibilities that lay outside, fascinated by the view it gave me, as well as both the sounds and smells of "movement!" That window became my place of solitude, where I could just be alone and imagine. I'd wonder about the conversations people engaged in as they walked and talked. I'd spend hours just contemplating where they were going as they rode together in cars or stood at the bus stop waiting to be picked up. When I wasn't gazing through that window, I could be found playing in the house with my siblings. From time to time, I'd find myself all alone on the side of the house on a self-made exploratory mission of what lay outside.

For some reason, I developed a love of the grass, plants, and all the things nature had to offer. I guess you could say

I was a very inquisitive little boy, always exploring my surroundings and just trying to figure things out. The constant thing, however, was rather in the house playing with my siblings, standing in the picture window gazing at the movement, or on an exploratory mission outside in the yard. I was always lost in my thoughts and imagination, trying to find "meaning."

Joseph Campbell once said, "The meaning of life is whatever you ascribe it to be. Being alive is the meaning."

In my thoughts, I was alive! I could be whoever I wanted to be. I was a superhero and the strongest, fastest one who ever lived! I guess that's why when I began pre-school, I fell in love with story time; the stories opened my imagination even further. I couldn't wait to learn how to read like the teacher so I could pick my own stories. I'd imagine myself right there in the book, going on the adventures the characters experienced. I had my mother, my siblings, a picture window to look out of, and now books! Life was amazing! Then one day, it all changed! As I sit, I can honestly say that the change began right at the picture window I used to look out of nearly every day.

*"Life is not made up of minutes, hours, days, weeks, months, or years, but of moments. You must experience each one before you can appreciate it."*

–SARAH BREATHNACH

# The Transitions of Life

My brothers and I were running through the house, playing as usual while Momma was at work. This time, we were sword fighting with broomsticks, and I, of course, was the superhero! As usual, when playing with boys, it got out of hand. I threw my stick at one of my brothers and broke Momma's picture window. I was devastated! I was the good guy! How could I have done such a thing? I spent the next few hours crying, ashamed of what I had done. When Momma came home and saw the broken window, she gave me something to cry about! For the first time, I felt the sting of a belt against my skin. It was at that point that I made up my mind that I didn't like it! I realized that the belt was what Momma had given to my brothers that made them cry. I made up my mind that I wouldn't do anything to make Momma use that belt on me again. I equate the breaking of that window with my change because, shortly after my first spanking, Momma came home from work one day, as usual. Only this time, she had someone with her. Momma called us all in the front room and announced to us, "This is your daddy!"

# Daddy

His name was Joseph Benjamin Pennington. Both my sister and oldest brother, who just so happened to be his namesake, already knew him! Though I was excited about the introduction, from the beginning, I felt strange because of the way he looked at me. Though I smiled at him as Momma used the word "daddy" for the first time, I could instantly—even at five years old—feel an uneasy sense of coldness coming from him as he looked back at me. Shortly after our introduction, his glare became clear. Daddy lined all six of us up from oldest to youngest and scolded us, saying, "Y'all not gonna run all over the house and you had better listen to Momma!" Then, while I was in the midst of thinking, *I always listen to Momma*, he grabbed me out of the line and said, "I heard about the window. Yo' butt is mine!"

Without hesitation, he took off his belt and hit me right in front of everybody! Through the screams of agony, I was confused because Momma didn't hit this hard. Furthermore, I'd already received a spanking for the window! Why was he hitting me so hard in front of everybody? More importantly, why was Momma letting him do that to me? Daddy grabbed my arm to hold me in the air while he hit me. I don't know how long it lasted. But when he finished, Daddy threw me to the floor, and he and Momma went down the hall to her bedroom. As I looked around the room, I could see that all my brothers and our sister were crying right along with me. Daddy was a terrifying man!

# Trauma

Researchers for The Center for Disease Control and Kaiser Permanente called events such as *My Meeting Daddy* Adverse Childhood Experiences (ACE). During their 17,000-participant survey, they found that ten ACEs of trauma impact most sufferers. People who have experienced more than one of these issues may struggle with what is called developmental trauma or sometimes complex trauma. The ten ACEs of trauma are forms of physical/emotional abuse, neglect, and household dysfunction, which include the following:

1. Physical abuse

2. Sexual abuse

3. Emotional abuse

4. Physical neglect

5. Emotional neglect

6. Mental illness

7. Divorce

8. Substance abuse

9. Violence against your mother

10. Having a relative who has been sent to jail or prison.

Even though I did everything possible to forget about the negative imprints of my early childhood to keep moving forward, I now understand that they affected every area of my life in every way possible.

A San Francisco therapist, Michael G. Quirke, MFT, once wrote, "Well, you know that you experienced some pretty difficult events during your childhood. However, you may have thought that, as an adult, you had moved past them. But deep down inside, you know this isn't true. That's because early life stresses change you on the inside."

So, imagine how a young man truly must feel on the inside who had experienced five of the ten listed before the age of six with abuse that just wouldn't stop.

## Trauma 2.0

Though we had explicit orders never to open the door for anyone when Momma wasn't home, every now and then, Daddy just popped up. Since he was Daddy, we always let him in.

For some reason, it seemed that as soon as he found out Momma wasn't home, he always made a beeline straight to me to slap me or whip me for no reason. That's why every time I saw him get out of his car from my pictured window, I yelled as loud as I could, "Daddy's here!" Then, I'd run to the back of the house to hide. The truth is I was terrified of Daddy.

Though the abuse wasn't always strictly mine alone, he seemed particularly more aggressive when it came to me. His routine was sometimes the same as that of a drill instructor. He'd line us up, from oldest to youngest, and walk before us, scolding us for something. Surprisingly, Daddy spoke softly. So, I'd watch and lean in closer to make sure I could hear every word. I had to make sure I wouldn't do whatever he was talking about so as to keep myself out of trouble. Every now and then, he'd end up slapping one of us from time to time (mostly me). Then, he would pull someone out of line and say, "Bend!" before whipping them while the rest stood there powerlessly, crying with every blow. Then, when he was done, Daddy would leave.

One day, Daddy stopped by when Momma wasn't home. He slapped me so hard that my ears were ringing. After he left this time, I went into the back room and cried to sleep. Though Daddy's drop-byes were sporadic, I had tried everything I knew to make sure I followed the directions he gave the last time he was there. In my mind, all I had to do was be good, and I'd win him over. Since my plan obviously did not work, I concluded that Daddy treated me like that because he just didn't like me, and that crushed my very soul. You see, I existed to make people happy, or at least that's what I thought.

Until then, I was always smiling, giving big hugs, and doing whatever I could to make Momma's day easier when she came home from work. I enjoyed the look on her face when I helped. Now, I was heartbroken. No matter how hard I tried to make Daddy see me for who I was, he just didn't like me. I was sure of it. I felt as though something was wrong with me. It was as though, somehow, my very presence irritated him. No matter how much I tried to show I was a loving child, Daddy rejected me.

When Momma got home from work that night, she found me still crying in my sleep and woke me up to see what was wrong. I was frightened, but I told Momma I'd been crying because Daddy just didn't like me. I told her everything he had been doing to me when he came by when she wasn't home. I could see in her eyes that she was furious! The next day, Momma had us all in the room and told us not to open the door for Daddy anymore. This was fine with me, especially considering the circumstances.

Sometime later, Daddy made one of his pop-ups. But this time, Momma was home. When we woke her up to tell her that Daddy was banging on the door again, she went down the stairs and opened the door for him. Once he came through the doorway into the small hallway at the bottom of the stairs, Momma closed the door behind him and attacked him! Without so much as a warning, she hit and kicked him while telling him not to touch her babies! Watching Momma in action defend me returned the sense of security I'd lost after meeting Daddy. He was trying to get away by running up the stairs, but Momma pulled him back down and gave him some more. Daddy's defense was to curl up into a ball until Momma got tired and told him to get out. He stopped dropping by for a long time. Then, one night, Momma came home from work, and guess who was with her … Daddy!

His actions toward me changed when he started coming by again. The truth is, however, I wish he would have kept up the personal abuse because, after that, instead of him hitting me, he made a game out of it. He had my older brothers hit me, which ultimately created an atmosphere where they did it while he wasn't there. On one occasion, though I can't remember what I did, he made me stand in the corner with my face to the wall, arms out to the side. He told me I would get a whopping if I dropped them. After some time, one of my brothers whispered in my ear, "Daddy is gone." When I put my arms down to both rest and wipe my face, there he was with the belt, accompanied by my brothers, who were laughing at me while he spanked me. There were also many times when one of my older siblings would either jump me or make my two younger brothers fight me after giving them broomsticks as weapons. They made a game out of it and would sometimes reward them with cookies at the end, telling them they had done a good job because they stuck together, even in defeat. On occasions, my younger brother held me down to punch and kick me after I had apparently hurt one of them badly while defending myself. I always won because I developed a strategy of attacking the weakest link full force, rendering him helpless and forcing the other to fight me one-on-one. I learned to endure the effects of the stronger brother while punishing the weaker. I was fueled by the motivation that, once I put one down for good, I'd have the opportunity to get my licks back from the other with reckless abandon! I developed this strategy because, when Momma got home, I would try to tell her; yet, for some reason, she wouldn't listen.

It was as though she refused to believe me and instead treated me as though I had become a little crybaby who would run to Momma just to get someone in trouble. To make her believe what was happening to me, I even tried not to wash my face sometimes so she could see the dried blood from the nosebleed they had given me. She only told me how nasty that was and made me wash my face. One day, I just got tired of being the victim. I made a promise to myself. "I will always get my lick back!"

My happy little world was beginning to crumble, and it all started the day I broke that window!

Life, for me, had now transitioned from feeling safe as long as I was with my family to a sense of loneliness. I never knew what would happen to me. I felt as invisible as the two-year-old sitting on the pallet while my mother gave birth. Only this time, that feeling wouldn't go away. The only time I truly felt seen was when I was in school listening to the teacher. I was now a big boy in the first grade at Angel Elementary School. I was totally in love with the place because they smiled, read to me, and, most of all, fed me.

Then, one day, Momma came home and told us that she had a surprise for us. She announced that we would be moving because she had bought us a home!

# My Foundation

*"Failure is the foundation of success and the means by which it is achieved. Success is the lurking place of failure, but who can tell when the turning point will come?"*

–LAO TZU

## Crocuslawn

C rocuslawn is the place where I can honestly say I truly began to become me! It was a single-family home sitting in the middle of a block filled with families and children of all ages. We must have moved into our new home in the summer because my earliest memories were of us using the driveway as a track where we'd race up and down it with Momma. Some of the elders in the neighborhood would block off the street on both sides and open the fire hydrant from time to time to allow us kids to play in the street. There was a fruit truck that would periodically come, and Momma would buy fresh fruits and vegetables. Sometimes, the "Playmobile or Swim mobile" came to the neighborhood for the neighborhood kids to enjoy. Our house was in the perfect spot. The setup was always in front of it because the fire hydrant was sitting at the curve at the end of the driveway on the left side. Life was off to a great start on Crocuslawn … until it was not. We now had a home; yet, life soon began to show the pain that came with the joy of homeownership. To put it nicely, we were "po" without the additional "or!" To sustain the household bills, Momma spent the majority of her time at work, which caused us kids to raise ourselves.

The year was 1976, and I was going to the second grade at George Washington Carver Elementary School. As I take a step back and look at the situation, while oblivious to the eight-year-old me, it is crystal clear that, with six children under twelve years old, Momma needed help!

According to the United States Census Bureau, the median income of all families in the US in 1979 was $19,680. More shockingly, there were about 25.2 million persons below the poverty level that year, constituting 11.6 percent of the U.S. population. It's important to note that 25.8% of those living below the poverty level were African Americans in Michigan cities.

## Poverty

There is an unforgettable stench of poverty known only to those who've experienced its atmosphere as a foundation. We smell hopelessness and hunger, distress and disease, desperation and despair. Most African Americans in poverty live in ghettos assumed by the majority as simply dangerous places where its occupants are degenerates preying on one another. The truth, however, is that impoverished communities are actually filled with proud people, full of love, bonded by a common struggle, most of which is the result of systematic oppression. Where an outsider sees hopelessness, there is an eerie sense of safety for those birthed within these communities who are bonded by the battle. The love in poverty is difficult to explain to those who don't live in poverty. We unconsciously use the smell of it to navigate our day-to-day lives. The time spent on Crocuslawn was filled with hunger, darkness, and cold winters, but we kids learned to survive. We'd ask our neighbors for food, turn the lights back on at the meter on the back of the house, and use the electric stove to turn the snow into water for drinking and bathing during the winter.

We were a family of seven, and though our house didn't run like others, we seemed to be doing just fine. My siblings and I always found a way to figure things out. We became accustomed to Momma not being home. We went for days without eating. For me, going to school was the easiest way I could think of to make sure I always had something to eat until summer break. I made sure I asked my teacher if I could go to the bathroom just to stop by one of their lockers to help myself to one of their lunches on the way. I distinctly remember my third-grade teacher talking to the entire class about how taking lunch from someone's locker was not only stealing but also causing the other kid to go hungry. That same day, there were two lunches at my frequent feeding spot because the parent obviously made an extra, just in case. Instead of taking the extra, I left both and decided to never make another kid hungry like me. It was that same third-grade teacher, however, who gave me my first *experience*, which made me aware that I wasn't like most of the other children who lived in the neighborhood where our school bus dropped us off.

We had a career day where we were assigned to do a poster board of what we wanted to be when we grew up. While I don't remember what any other kid presented as a project, I do recall how proud I was about mine. I stood in front of my class, proudly presented my poster, and declared to all that I wanted to be the President of the United States of America. At the end, the teacher looked at me and told me as I stood there in front of the entire class, "That won't happen because there has never been a Black president."

Nobody had ever told me I was Black before, nor that Black people couldn't be what they wanted to be. I was not only embarrassed; I was devastated!

During the summers, my older brothers fed us with bags of cookies or chips they stole from one of our neighborhood grocery stores. Sometimes, the neighbors brought us meals. My brothers showed us at an early age how to steal food for the family and clothes for us to wear from Kingsway. The first time it was my turn to get a meal for the family, I was so frightened. I just put the first thing I got under my coat and ran out of the store. When I got home, my brothers instantly ridiculed me because I had brought home one can of beans and franks to feed six people. Though we ate it, they all agreed I was absolutely terrible at getting food for the family. They never sent me again. This was fine with me because I didn't want to do it anyway! My brothers and I laugh about this incident to this very day.

Another part of what I would call my "training" was how my brothers entertained themselves while we were stuck in the house while Momma was at work. By this time, I had become a victim in my own home, used for the amusement of others. My older brothers either knocked me around to make me fight them, or they made my younger brothers fight me for the cookies or chips we had as our dinner. Those fights quickly became unfair. Neither could beat me one-on-one, so they would make the other "help their brother out." They'd sometimes even hold me down while they kicked and stomped me because I always found a way to overcome the odds. The crazy thing, though, is no matter how much I was tortured at home, nobody outside the house was ever allowed to mess with any of us. I loved my brothers; they loved me, and nothing could ever stop that.

Though life began to be noticeably difficult, we still had each other. As mentioned earlier, Joe and Pat (though not even teenagers at the time) became our teachers of what I now call our "survival training." They'd sit us all down in a circle and instruct us how to get food, keep warm, and, most of all, protect ourselves from outsiders. As an elementary school student, I learned how to wear loose-fitting clothing to go "grocery shopping" to feed the family using the oversized pants legs to conceal the "grocery" items. It was during those sessions that I also learned how to fight!

I truly believe my older siblings forcing my younger brothers to double-team me was a byproduct of what Daddy used to make them do to me. Well, it turned out that I became pretty good at defending myself. When they started giving them broomsticks as weapons, unless one of them decided to jump in, somehow, I always came out on top. These times took my innocence away, as I became a distant little boy who could be extremely mean when provoked and developed a reputation for refusing to let people touch me. Deep down, I hated being that way. However, I had grown weary of being terrorized in my home by those whom I loved with no one to protect me. I can't remember when it happened, but I made up my mind one day that no matter who it was, I'd always get my "lick" back, even if it took a few days. I spent my alone hours practicing situations in my head and rehearsing how to make sure I won a fight. To make sure that I didn't lose the edge, I often found a reason to get into a fight with somebody to sharpen my skills. I got so good that my brothers would take me to street fights and put me up against others who were known to be good fighters. To this day, I've never lost a street fight.

I was in my formative years, having siblings who ganged up on me, a mother who was always at work, and a daddy who was simply useless. Daddy *never* attempted to provide for us. He made no effort to raise his growing boys, and he never came to see how anybody but Momma was doing. Then, there was a man named Desmond Moore. I don't know when it happened, but I remember meeting my younger brother's father, Desmond Moore, whom everyone affectionately called Dez. He just popped up one day when we lived on Crocuslawn to see Momma.

# Desmond Moore

Dez was a really tall man with a deep voice whom we all loved. He treated all of us like we were his children. Not to mention, unlike Daddy, he never laid a hand on any of us! Momma was either in love with both Dez and Daddy or just enjoyed both of their "room meetings" from time to time since that's where both spent most of the time whenever they came over. There was a significant difference between the two of them. Dez seemed kind and would sit and talk to us when he came over before he went into the room with Momma. Daddy, on the other hand, was cold and never seemed to care about anything concerning us. He rarely, if ever, even acknowledged my presence.

One day, Daddy came to the house and gave all of us a whooping for who knows what. Yet, this time, we all came to the same conclusion that we wanted Dez, not Daddy. The next time Dez came over, during his talk with us kids, I told him Daddy came over from time to time. Then either Joe or Pat told him that Daddy had been whooping Jamel and Dwight (who, as it turned out, were actually his children). Dez didn't stay long that time because he and Momma got into a heated argument about what we told him, which apparently made him furious. Someday later, when Daddy came over, Dez popped up. Only this time, he hadn't come to see Momma! I don't know who let him in while Daddy was upstairs in Momma's room, but Dez had a machete with him. He came in yelling, "Where you at?! You don't ever put your hands on my kids!"

Momma came out of the room and ran downstairs, trying to hold Dez back as he attempted to get upstairs to deal with Daddy. She kept pleading with him, trying to calm him down, but Dez didn't have any of it. I distinctly remember hearing the sound of Daddy's car speeding off as Dez finally got past Momma and started up the stairs. It turns out that, during the commotion, Daddy had tied the sheets in Momma's room together on one end and tied them around the waist of my sister Rosa. He had her brace her feet against the walls and hold them while he climbed out the upstairs bedroom window. My brothers and I laugh about this incident today because it turned out that Daddy wanted absolutely no part of Dez. Though Momma acted like his stopping by to jump on Daddy wasn't right, we loved every second of it!

Finding out Daddy was actually a coward removed the fear of him from us. This became evident when my oldest brother was 11 or 12 and got into a fistfight with Daddy in the living room. He was winning the battle until Daddy bent his fingers back and ultimately subdued him due to the pain. I can still hear Joe screaming. "But I'm just a little boy!"

Daddy responded, "You weren't a little boy a few minutes ago!"

An incident that should have traumatized a child actually gave me hope. When my brother grabbed Daddy during the original tussle and body-slammed him to the floor, it was as if I was helping him lift Daddy into the air.

After Momma finished talking to Dez about coming to the house with a machete, he came out of the room and spent some time with us, although I could see he had been crying. Dez may have only been the father of Jamel and Dwight, but it was evident that he genuinely cared for all of us. Unlike Daddy, I felt safe in his presence and often showed it by running into his big arms every time he stopped by for a visit. Unfortunately, Dez's visits became less frequent after he made Daddy climb out the window. When he stopped by after that, he came to spend time with us kids and never went into the room with Momma anymore.

Daddy stopped coming for a while, too. When he started coming back on a regular basis, he neither parked in front of the house nor in the driveway. Instead, his car could always be found a few houses down or across the street. He visited our neighbor and his mom from time to time when Momma wasn't home. Though his beatings slimmed down somewhat, sometimes he'd stop by and sit under a blanket with my sister for a while if neither the neighbor nor Momma was home. While we never talked about it, we knew exactly what Daddy was doing to Rosa under that blanket.

Then, one day, I smelled smoke again. But this time, none of us were in the house! While I never knew exactly how the fire started, there was a rumor on the streets that our home had been firebombed. Without hesitation, we ended up in foster care *again*! Yet, this time, something good came out of it.

# Foster Care 2.0

I remember the name Ozell Knuckles!

She was as mean as a junkyard dog and, unfortunately, was our foster mother! Ms. Ozell would yell at us and whip my older brothers every chance she got. We told Momma about it during our visits with her. But, for some reason, she didn't do anything about it. Then, one day, Ms. Ozell decided she was gonna whip one of my older brothers for something. Yet, this time, Pat and Joe had already decided they would defend one another. When all the commotion was over, my older brothers ran away from the foster care home, which caused a bigger problem. Then, out of nowhere, within a few weeks after they ran away, Momma showed up on Ozell's porch with an older gentleman with smooth black skin like me, dressed to the tee, who happened to be driving a Cadillac.

As he took off his hat, Momma, beaming proudly to those of us left in Ozell's house, said, "This is your grandfather!"

# The Sense of Self-Awareness

## My Granddaddy

H is name was George Wadley, Sr., and he was born in Sardis, Mississippi. He was the only son of Thorton Wadley and Rosa Caldwell Wadley. It appears that Granddaddy left home when he was a young man and later started a family with his first wife, who bore him three daughters (Mercedes, Anne, and Georgia). From what I learned through the years, my grandfather was a butcher by trade and bore the scars on his now deformed hands from his craft after years of work. After his first break-up, Granddaddy moved to Detroit to work in the meat markets. He met a woman named Louise Quinn, who bore him three children: Loretta (my mother), George, Jr., and Flora. Though I had no idea why this was the first time I had ever met him, I later found out that the family had become estranged after my Grandma Louise died because none of his children accepted the woman Granddaddy got involved with, who eventually became his third wife, Rita. As a matter of fact, Momma had not even spoken to her daddy since it was rumored that he married Rita, who bore his seventh child, Nicole, around 1974, which happened to be six years after I was born. Tragedy has a way of bringing family together, if just for a little while, since we were meeting our granddaddy for the first time!

I instantly loved my Granddaddy. I followed him around everywhere he went. He bought me a suit because I made sure I went to the Kingdom Hall with him every time he stepped out of the door. I sat and listened to the stories they told about somebody named Jehovah. I was just starting to read well, but I became fascinated with the pictures in the books they had. I made sure I read the pamphlets we passed out as we went door to door through the streets of Kalamazoo. For the first time in a long time, I felt safe, seen, and loved.

I could have stayed with them forever. But one day, Momma took us back to Detroit, moving us into her friend's house while our home was still being repaired from the fire. Though I cried like a little baby because I didn't want to go, Momma picked us up because it appeared there was an argument between the adults.

When we arrived in Kalamazoo, we kids were split between Grandad's and our Aunt Flora's, Momma's little sister, who just so happened to live in the area. Apparently, Aunt Flora was having trouble trying to care for three additional children while struggling to care for her own son, especially considering Momma was back in Detroit kid-free! Aunt Flora had recently divorced from an abusive husband and was already troubled as a single parent. Then, there was Grandma Rita, who absolutely wasn't signing up to care for all six children of a woman who wouldn't so much as say, "Hello" to her when she walked into her house. On top of that, it was evident Momma never even accepted the daughter that Grandad and Rita had. While Momma didn't consider her a sister, that little girl was my Auntie Nicole.

I was absolutely crushed when we left! I had just met the kindest man in the world, who happened to be my grandaddy and the sweetest little girl on the planet. Just like that, they were being taken away from me.

It still breaks my heart. The next time I laid eyes on Grandaddy and Auntie Nicole, my aunt was married with a child of her own.

I returned to the old neighborhood and eventually was promoted into middle school for my sixth-grade year, where I began attending Charles R. Drew Middle School.

As we got older, life back in our home on Crocuslawn went from bad to worse. My older siblings were now teenagers and had graduations, per se, of their own. They had now graduated from the occasional shoplifting as a means of providing food for the family to B&E's, robberies, and anything else that could get them whatever they felt was needed.

As for me, the school had switched from being my sanctuary to now becoming a place filled with young people trying to make a name for themselves in between classes. I found myself in a place filled with different cliques, and I somehow fell right in line with them. Apparently, my reputation had infiltrated my safe place because the street fights I was famous for had made themselves known to Drew. I battled in between classes for the amusement of the hall or "pod" that we were assigned to. I was assigned to the "blue hall" and was often put up against the "tough kid" from the green or yellow hall. Though I always won, I hated every fight. It was apparent that fighting became my identity. Unfortunately, at this stage of my life, it was the only thing I was good at.

Due to the torture I received from my brothers at home, I had now become the neighborhood boy known for putting a whipping on anyone who touched me. Nobody knew, but the inside amusement of my family was now displayed for the entire neighborhood.

My brothers put me up against bigger kids in the neighborhood, whom I would fight for bragging rights or to settle arguments between families. The Penningtons had become so unruly that the only children that neighborhood parents allowed to play with us were the Ester Boys: Robert, Michael, LaNard, and Ervin. The Ester boys were similar in age to us. They had two older sisters and were also all being raised by a single mother. The Esters and Penningtons became all we had, so we were connected at the hip.

I rolled and smoked my first joint, stole my first bike, and made my first decision to protect others with Nard—all before I was twelve years old! Nard and I were thick as thieves until my little brother Jamel beat the brakes off of his little brother, Ervin. We became distant because Nard wanted to avenge his little brother. Still, he knew I absolutely wasn't going to let that happen. Our older brothers wanted to see us go at it, but he and I had an unspoken vow never to fight one another.

Life at that time was chaotic, and I was going with the flow like a dead fish. I despised the constant fighting, hunger, and lack of genuine people who actually cared. But I was a kid and, therefore, I was powerless. Though surrounded by the chaos of existence while participating in most of the shenanigans, at ten years old, I concluded that I wanted nothing to do with the way I was living.

As I walked during my alone time, thinking about my situation, I declared repeatedly: "I won't be nothing like them!"

Having spent most of my time alone, I always talked to myself. Yet, this is the first time I remember that I meant exactly what I said. Don't get me wrong, I loved Momma and my siblings, but I couldn't stand the atmosphere of life in that home. I wanted to be with my family; yet, I wanted us to be safe, loved, supported, and most of all, *free*. For some reason, I was afraid to let my true feelings be known. I knew I was different. Yet, I understood I was not better. I was simply different.

And ... "I won't be nothing like them!"

*"Affirmations help build and improve your self-esteem. They can also act as a way of challenging and replacing your negative and anxious thinking when it comes to stress, depression, physical pain, and anxiety."*

–LEE PHILLIPS, LCSW, EDD

No one truly knew how out of control our life was until a few of the neighbors finally reached their breaking point. One day, my oldest brother Joe was playing a video game at our neighborhood party store when two of our neighbors who lived in the corner house confronted him about the beating he had put on their son with a twelve-inch section of a water hose he had made. The man snatched Joe off the game he was playing because he was ignoring them as they were yelling.

Furious that an adult had actually grabbed him, Joe came home and told us what had happened, and both he and Pat ran back to the store to deal with them. When it was all over, Joe had knocked the man out in the middle of Chicago. Pat had broken a two by four across the head of his wife as she attempted to help her husband get up. Joe was fifteen, Pat was thirteen, and I was almost twelve years old. That night, as I slept on our couch that sat against the living room window, I was suddenly awakened by gunshots.

While I always thought that the couple that my brothers had retaliated against stood in front of our home to shoot up a house filled with children, I recently found out their son actually did the shooting. After what Joe had done to him, coupled with what transpired when his parents confronted him about it, he broke into his mother's room and took the weapons. My brother Pat actually saw him standing in front of the house when he went through the back door and made his way to the front.

As the bullets continued ringing out, some smashing through the window where I lay, I was frozen in terror as my brother Pat crawled to the couch and pulled me to the floor, covering me until the shooting stopped. While I never knew what happened to the young man who did this, what I do know is that when the police brought Momma home from work, she was *pissed*!

The stare that she gave Joe and Pat was the absolutely most death-defying look I have ever seen back then, and I haven't seen anything like it since. A few days later, Momma came home from work and took me on bus rides, eventually leading us to the east side of Detroit, where she opened the door to a three-bedroom apartment on the corner of East Jefferson and McClellan. Later, Momma brought my younger brothers Jamel and Dwight. Days turned into weeks for the four of us until I realized that she didn't bring any of my other siblings to the apartment.

Instead, she left my sister Rosa (who was seventeen) at her boyfriend's house, whom she had basically been living with anyway. She left Joe (who was fifteen) and Pat (who was thirteen) right at the home they had caused to get shot up. I know now that Momma did that to save her younger children. Sometime later, I found out that Momma eventually bought two one-way bus tickets, placing them in individually labeled envelopes that she gave to the next-door neighbor for my brothers. Pat had an envelope with a bus ticket to Kalamazoo and my granddaddy's address, while Joe's had a ticket to Georgia with the name Georgia Wadley written on a piece of paper. The craziest thing about those tickets is that Momma neither asked nor told her father or her older sister that she was shipping her sons to them.

While Pat at least was somewhat familiar with who he was sent to, and he spent the rest of his teenage years in the Kalamazoo/Portage area, Joe landed in an unfamiliar place where he tells the story of someone at the bus station knowing Aunt Georgia who gave him a ride to her house. Unfortunately, according to him, Aunt Georgia had mental issues. She was unable to take care of herself, so it was absolutely impossible to care for him. After some time, Joe made his way back to Detroit and became a member of the Young Boys Incorporated (YBI). YBI was the infamous drug ring that was led by Richard Wershe, Jr., better known as "White Boy Rick." Though he tried to come back home many times, Momma wouldn't let him. Momma's brother, my Uncle George, let Joe live with him for a while. But he put him out after Joe beat him up for beating on his wife.

Though Joe didn't live with us, he was always around to protect us. He sold drugs on the eastside, where he became known as *ICE* after becoming security for well-known drug dealers.

# Survival of the Fittest

*"It's not the strongest of the species that survives nor the most intelligent that survives. It is the one that is most adaptable to change."*
−CHARLES DARWIN

## Eastside

I was now the big brother. However, the only thing I liked about it was knowing that I finally had a chance to get my licks back for all the times my younger brothers were forced to gang up on me. The thought of being able to get them back sounded good. But deep down, I knew I would never harm either of them. Instead, I took on the role of protector, just as my older brothers had previously been for us. The three of us were in an unfamiliar environment. Nobody knew us, and we knew nobody. Neither did we tell the kids in the neighborhood that we were running from the westside of Detroit after adults tried to kill us. Jamel, Dwight, and I were quiet and usually remained to ourselves. Still, the neighborhood kids quickly found out that I would beat the brakes off of anybody who so much as said something out of the way to one of us. I decided early on that the best way for people to leave you alone was to find the neighborhood bully and simply put a knot upside his head while everybody was watching. Nobody messed with you after that. I had the chance to "reinvent myself," and I took the opportunity to do just that.

I began the seventh grade at Butzel Jr. High School on Van Dyke and Kercheval, which was about a 30-40-minute walk from the house, depending on the weather. When Momma took me into the office to register me for school, I distinctly remember the lady asking me if I considered myself a smart student or if I had challenges. I looked directly at that lady and proudly proclaimed, "I'm a smart kid!" She made that comment because when she reviewed my last report card, it was filled with A's and B's, but it had a big fat D in drafting! She had no idea that I had an altercation with my sixth-grade drafting teacher, who kept calling me *"Desington"* as he took attendance every day. One day, I had just about enough of this white man continuing to mispronounce my name on purpose every day. I was a quiet kid in class because I hated attention. But this time, I yelled out, "My name is Des! How would you like me to call you Honkeyton?!"

As laughter riddled out from the kids in class, he ordered me to stand in the hallway and wait until he came out.

While I proudly strolled to the hallway feeling vindicated, I knew he would never mispronounce my name again and that I wasn't gonna pass his class. The strangest thing happened when the teacher met me in the hallway. He stared right through me as he walked toward the spot I stood in. Once my teacher got close, he took out a book and silently read to himself for about five to ten minutes. He never said a word to me. At the end of the time, with the same look he had as he initially approached me in the hallway, he said, "You can go back to class if you want to, or you don't ever have to come back. Either way, I don't care."

I had no idea what kind of pressure the teacher was under being a Caucasian man attempting to teach in a school filled with unruly kids that didn't look like him. Nor did he know that I was a kid in turmoil and in desperate need of someone to care. Since he made it perfectly clear that he didn't, neither did I. My D was a result of my lack of even a simple attempt at trying in that class. The funny thing is that I still struggle with creating drawings to communicate how things function or are constructed. Even when using a ruler, I have yet to develop a way to make straight lines.

According to the Heuristic Encyclopedia, *imprinting* is the process by which certain childhood or adolescent experiences impact an individual so significantly that these memories bear a governing influence over their adult identity and behavior. Imprinting hard wires our brain at a developmental age, subsequently evolving and affecting our decisions and behaviors later in life. As I write this, I realize that this incident caused a mental block that has affected me for the rest of my life.

Another thing that had a major imprint on my life during my developmental years was how I was introduced to sex. I had already had multiple "experiences" from one of my sister's much older friends making me "hump" her whenever she had Rosa bring me with her to visit when I was about five or six years old. One day while exploring the eastside apartment building Momma had moved us to, my twelve-year-old self turned the knob of an unlocked door to an unoccupied apartment and received the shock of my life.

This room was filled with pornographic magazines depicting some of the most grotesque actions anybody could ever imagine! Encapsulated, I spent hours in that room trying to thumb through every page of the thousands of magazines, being hypnotized day after day. I didn't realize that, with each flip of a page, I was formulating an unrealistic view of sex. Then, one day, I went to my secret room to spend time with my stash, and they were all gone.

Though someone had found and taken them all away, I spent decades of my life searching for the euphoria found in that room, battling the internal demons that had planted seeds of promiscuity, lust, and unrealistic views of intimacy in my mind. I was on a new side of town, in a new school, developing old habits that would be hard to break.

At Butzel, I had a chance to show the teachers that I was a smart kid, and I didn't get Ds.

One day after the first card marking, I was taken out of the original class that I had been placed in and transferred into a new classroom. I soon found out that Butzel's administration decided to create a class filled with the brightest seventh graders in the school. That's where I met a guy who would become my lifelong best friend, Maurice G. Morton.

I actually became friends with his older brother Lawrence, who was in the class I was initially placed in. Lawrence actually introduced me to Maurice when he told me that his younger brother was put into our newly formed class. I never questioned how he was in the same grade as his younger brother, not even after meeting Maurice's twin, Terrell.

I spent the rest of that year watching Maurice's every move. I was fascinated that he wasn't like any of the kids I knew. At eleven years old, this guy was focused. He was concerned about his appearance and was competitive in every subject in the classroom. He would articulate who he was and what he would become at the drop of a dime. He made sure that he only surrounded himself with the good kids. He had no problem having a "discussion" with you if he felt like you were slipping in your grades. Early on, I realized that I would be his protector because he couldn't fight, and one of these kids was going to jump him for something he said one day. It turned out that we both lived on Belvidere Street after we moved into a house around the corner from the apartment building Momma brought us to. Same street. Only the Mortons lived between Mack and Gothey while the Penningtons resided between Agnes and E. Jefferson, five blocks down the street.

We often walked home together down Kercheval, where he'd go right, and I'd go left when we got to Belvidere. Though I only spent the night one time, I truly loved spending time at the Mortons. His mother and father were married and had thirteen kids, all of whom they raised in that house, which is the reason I couldn't spend the night. I absolutely adored Momma Morton, who was a homemaker. I honored Papa Morton, who was a professional man who worked tirelessly to take care of his family. Sometimes, I'd sit and talk to Papa or Momma Morton while Maurice and his brothers were outside because they made me feel like part of the family. Though we lived on the same street, they had no idea how much turmoil I had experienced at such a young age.

The Clays were another family on Belvidere, and I frequently could be found in their house. I'm not sure how we met. But their oldest son, John, and I were the same age, so we walked to school together. He had three younger brothers (and later a baby sister) and two parents in the home. Their father, John Sr., worked at Ford Motor Company. Their mother, Betty Clay, was a homemaker who happened to be the most Christian woman I had ever met. She could cook like the gods. I always conveniently wound up at their house at dinner time because I knew she would feed me. I was there so much that, after dinner, she would sometimes assign me to wash or dry the dishes, just like her own kids. I credit Betty Clay as the person who actually sparked my curiosity concerning who God was, as she took me to church with her family on Sunday mornings. Momma had taken us to the Catholic churches in the neighborhoods we lived in. I had both received my first communion, as well as become an altar boy at Annunciation Catholic Church on Agnes. But going to a Baptist church filled with people who looked like me, who seemed to have so much enthusiasm about God, made me feel more at home. I never joined that church; however, I continued to join the Clays at their dinner table almost every night. I don't think they ever realized that being at the Clays' table kept my hunger to a minimum and, more importantly, kept me from stealing to feed myself.

While I didn't realize it at the time, I began the development of not only my desire for a family, but also my feelings about how a family was to operate. Both the

Mortons and Clays had a working father, who served as the breadwinner for the household, and a loving mother who cared for every aspect of the home up to and including the nurturing and feeding of the family. The love of the children by both parents would be evident as the father would often be seen playing with his kids in the summertime or on weekends when he wasn't working. Still, momma was where the kids received most of their love and support. I often fantasized about being in such a home, losing myself in my thoughts from time to time and, on occasion, shaking myself to make sure I didn't become jealous of my buddies for what they had. I recall even almost beating the brakes off of my friend John Clay, Jr. for getting mad at his mother for not buying him a blue jean jumpsuit for Easter one year. How dare he talk to me behind his mother's back when she did *everything* for him! The truth is I grew closer to my friends' mothers than them in many ways over the years because, secretly, I wished they were mine.

When we moved to the east side, I only saw Daddy twice:

- One time, he came to the apartment on Jefferson, where Momma told him never to come back because she was dating a man named Reggie.

- The other time was when I saw him parked by the apartment, and he let me sit in his car, where we talked for the first time.

Sitting in the back of his car with him and asking how Momma was doing was the first real conversation he and I ever had. As morbid as that sounds, the truth is I really liked it. Somewhere between the shooting and her new boyfriend, Reggie, she had made up her mind that she was done entirely with Daddy. As we talked, I could tell he was truly hurt by Momma finally cutting him off, even though we found out that he had been married all along a few years before our house got shot up.

Daddy had apparently married the lady his mother wanted for him before he and Momma married. From what I understand, Momma and her mother-in-law were like dynamite and a spark: incapable of being in the same vicinity at the same time. Daddy was a momma's boy. So, when he and Momma got into disagreement, he was welcomed into his momma's home with open arms. My grandfather was the one who told me that every time Momma got pregnant, Daddy would say the baby wasn't his. He'd run home to his momma, who'd gladly let him stay with her until after Momma gave birth and forgave him.

Someone also told me Momma and Granddaddy had actually fallen out after Momma tried to attack him the night her mother, my Grandma Lousie, died. This was before I was born, but Momma had to be sedated and was sent away for some time after Granny's death. To make matters worse, my Grandma Lousie had a best friend named Mabel Moore, who lived a few doors down. The two of them raised their children together. Like most African American families, because their children were raised together, her best friend became Aunt Mabel, which means the children were considered cousins. Well, Desmond, who was my two younger brothers' father, was Mabel's son. Momma had two kids by her "cousin!"

This is why Daddy and Desmond knew each other and, more importantly, why we were estranged from our extended family. I found out years later that not only were Desmond and Momma raised as cousins, but he was married and had two other boys with his wife, whom my younger brothers have never met to this day. Their "secret" affair not only birthed two children, but Momma also named her last baby, Des, who was born prior to divorcing her husband, which happens to have been the nickname everybody calls him. Since I knew that the two of them divorced shortly after my birth, I was convinced from that moment on that Daddy didn't like me because Momma named me after her boyfriend.

My "family fantasies" were just about being normal!

# Becoming an Adult

## High School Years

**W**hen we became eighth graders, Maurice came to me one day and told me we didn't need to go to Martin Luther King when we graduated. Instead, he convinced me to apply to the college preparatory high school known as Cass Technical High School because it would "prepare us for college." I knew nothing about Cass Tech, and college was the last thing on my mind. I was concerned about how I would survive the next day while he was thinking about what he would be doing five years from then. I didn't want to let him down, however, so I completed the application, and we were both accepted.

Once I arrived in the hallways of the ninth grade at Cass, I went from a class with *one Maurice* to an entire school of Maurices. But this time, he and I only had one class together. For the first time, I was concerned with my appearance. There were literally thousands of kids everywhere. Daily, it was a fashion show. I didn't want any of my new classmates to make me put a knot upside their heads for talking about me. So, I took the clothes I could fit to the neighborhood laundromat, where I'd do my homework while washing. Because I didn't have much, I figured out I could wear the same pair of blue jeans at least three times a week:

- Day 1: Blue jeans with any color shirt

- Day 2: Same jeans with a different shirt

- Day 3: Same jeans, different shirt with jacket, sweater, or some other cover

I sometimes got a fourth wear out of my jeans by wearing them inside out as a fashion statement. The crazy thing is that my classmates had no idea how much I was struggling, and I never volunteered the information.

While the neighborhood high school was only about a mile up Jefferson, Cass Tech was more than five miles away from my house, which caused me to have to take the bus to school every day. Since Momma had stopped working for some reason, and she didn't always have $5.50 per week, it cost me to get to school. At fourteen years old, I collected bottles and cans to return to the store, picked up a neighborhood paper route, and sometimes ran store errands for some of the neighbors to make sure I didn't miss school. When I was short, I'd often catch the bus to school but walk home. It didn't matter to me because I became lost in the artistry of the city, dreaming of one day being free while making positive affirmations of how I'd live my life when I made it.

I transitioned to the neighborhood hustler that many of the neighbors would assist because they knew I was a smart kid just trying to do something with myself. I could often be found sitting on somebody's front porch with one of the elders, expressing that I wanted to be a doctor and asking them if they needed me to go to the store or do something for them. I always respected older people because they seemed to have so much wisdom. They were actually concerned and seemed to enjoy my company since they didn't always have visitors. I even stopped fighting so much because one of them would often tell me how disappointed they were when they found out I had whipped somebody's kid.

One day, while in school, I befriended this tall, skinny kid named Liyongo Tolin. We had multiple classes together, and he reminded me of my younger brother Jamel. Since we were in the Chem-Bio curriculum at school, we were hanging pretty tough when Maurice linked his classes with ours after the second report card marking. The two quickly became four because Maurice met another kid named Marc Oliver Rapley, who shared multiple classes with him at the beginning of the year. For the first time, I became somewhat popular in school by hanging out with them at the place where I even got a girlfriend.

Life at Cass was off to a great start. I spent my time lost in my classroom studies and newfound circle of friends so much that it actually made me forget about my home life. Then, one day, my life changed *forever*!

Momma broke up with Reggie, stopped working so many hours, and was almost always at home in her room. My sister Rosa and older brothers were now coming in and out of our house, and my younger brothers were busy living their own little lives. Though fractured, we were a family again … imperfect, yet we were surviving. One day, I saw an ambulance in front of our home, which was taking Momma to the hospital!

We were growing children so none of us spent daylight hours at home. It was a coincidence that my younger brother Jamel came home and found Momma lying on the floor in a pool of blood. We later found out that Momma had given birth to a stillborn child, though none of us even knew she was pregnant. From what I gather, the reason she had broken up with Reggie was because he got her pregnant and she absolutely wanted no more kids. Once she realized she was pregnant, instead of getting an abortion, she decided against prenatal visits and basically starved herself. Say what you want, but Momma wasn't about to bring another life into the world that she couldn't take care of. As harsh as this sounds, either I began to see a difference in

Momma after that because I was older and beginning to understand real life, or something snapped in Momma after that because she was never the same.

Her change became even more evident after the unfortunate incident that happened to me when I spent the night at a neighbor's house. There was a disabled man named Reggie (not Momma's ex) who was the neighborhood father to all the kids who were being raised by single parents. Though he got around using two crutches, and he wore a colostomy bag with an unforgettable stench because it had to be periodically changed, children who didn't have fathers often stayed around him. It was apparent that Reggie must have really wanted kids because he treated each and every one of them as if they were his own.

I met Reggie through my younger brother Jamel. He was one of Reggie's favorite kids, and my brother could always be found spending the night there. I grew fond of Reggie because he really took care of my little brother, which made Jamel light up each time he saw him. On a Friday, I decided to spend the night at Reggie's, as I had done on many occasions before. Still, he let me sleep upstairs because I wanted to watch the late-night marathon karate movies. After all, we didn't have a TV at home. Sometime during the night, I had apparently fallen asleep because I was awakened by a wet feeling on my backside and the voice of one of the adult friends of the family (George Hollifield) saying before passing out, "He can just button his pants up when he wakes up."

Reggie had sent a drunk man upstairs to *sleep it off*, forgetting I was already up there. At first, I thought it was all a dream. But when I went into the bathroom upstairs, my worst fears were valid. I stood in the mirror, numb. I was a fourteen-year-old boy known for defending himself. How could I let this happen? Why didn't I feel anything until after it was all over? Had I allowed my guard to be let down that low to please the elders in the neighborhood? More importantly, why was I not trying to kill him for what he did?

After I gathered myself, I went downstairs and asked Reggie who he had sent upstairs as I told him and Smokie (who was one of the neighborhood gangsters) what had just happened to me. Smokie grabbed his gun and was on his way upstairs to deal with George, but Reggie begged him to stop. They called the police, who took the man to jail when they arrived. As if the incident itself wasn't devastating enough, how my mother reacted pushed me into a dark place that I never truly recovered from. The Oxford Dictionary defines the word survival as the state or fact of continuing to live or exist, typically in spite of an accident, ordeal, or difficult circumstances. Momma and I sat in the interrogation room as a detective took my statement.

They had the perpetrator and all the evidence, including the sheets from the bed and the clothing I was wearing. Yet, it appeared they were more set on finding out if Reggie had set this all up, as if he had all those boys at his house for that reason. Absolutely *not*! Reggie never thought in a million years that some adult would mess with one of his boys. I talked to Reggie about the incident years later, and he was still devastated about what happened. He beat himself up until the day he died about it, even though I never blamed him for the incident. I doubt if he was as devastated as I was by my mother's comment when the detective finally left the room. Momma giggled when the detective left us alone in that room after concluding his interrogation. When I finally asked her why she was laughing, Momma whispered to me, "You better be glad he wasn't a black man!"

My abuser, being white, didn't send me into the abyss; it was the fact that my mother could be so cruel to find anything humorous about what had just occurred to her fourteen-year-old son.

I never looked at Momma or anybody else the same after that! Though I went to school Monday morning as if nothing had happened, something died in me that weekend. I didn't want anyone to pity me or look at me as though I were damaged goods. So, like everything else in my life, I forcibly mentally blocked it out. Anytime my mind steered toward that memory, I'd slap my hands against my head to snap myself out of it. I'd get up and go for a walk to dream about something else. If the feeling didn't leave, I'd often resort to violence just to make myself feel better about myself. Yet, for the most part, I stopped caring, stopped studying, and stopped trusting. I simply began going through the motions. I was existing without being present, refusing to let anything or anyone get the best of me.

I was truly changed *forever.*

According to the Cleveland Clinic, "Affirmations, also referred to as positive affirmations, are phrases that, when repeated regularly, can change negative thoughts and behavior patterns. These statements are usually intended to help shift thinking from negative to positive, motivate an action, reduce stress, persevere through difficult times, and increase self-confidence and well-being."

It was at this time that I began to accept the fact that I was truly alone in this world, even though people surrounded me. On my walks from school, I began to say, "If you would send me someone who would love me for me, I'll serve you for the rest of my life!"

I had no idea who I was talking to or when it started, but this was something I often said for as long as I could remember. It made me feel safe and at peace. Whenever I got down on myself or felt lonely, I'd repeat it.

I became mentally distant from everyone for the remainder of that school year. However, no one could really tell since, by this time, I had mastered the mask that I wore, which hid my inner turmoil. Sometime during the middle of the summer of that year, it hit me one day that I had been coming home to an empty house for quite some time. I was used to being by myself for multiple days in a row. But after the landlord asked me where Momma was because he needed his rent, I realized I hadn't seen Momma, nor my younger brothers, in a while.

After weeks of searching, I knocked on the door of one of the places my friend John Clay had taken her to for work a few times. When I rang the bell, Momma answered the door!

Though she seemed shocked to see me, she told me to go in the back room after I explained that the landlord wanted his money or us out. Much to my surprise, I walked into the backroom and found my little brothers comfortably sleeping. While I sat there stunned, trying to figure out what was happening, I heard Momma and the man arguing about my being there, upon which I heard something that resulted in the ripping of a hole in my soul.

"I don't care who he is! Get that *nigga* out my house!"

While the words from that white man caused damage to the already existing wound created by what happened earlier in the year at Reggie's house, the hole in my soul appeared when the woman who gave birth to me told me I had to leave! No matter the circumstances she may have been in at the time, she chose him over me, and I instantly hated her for it. I was helplessly broken at being discarded as if I were some used pieces of unwanted clothing. Where in the world was a fifteen-year-old boy supposed to go, and more importantly, how was I supposed to live? Though tears rolled down my face until there were none left, each drop made me cold, uncaring, unbothered. As despondent as I was, being rejected by the person I loved the most, eerily, I subconsciously made the decision that I would survive no matter what. Though angry beyond explanation, I would use this rejection, that anger, as my fuel, my protection, my comfort.

Fredrich Nietzsche once said, "He who has a why to live for can bear almost any how." Daddy hated me. Momma discarded me. My siblings treated me differently. So, "F' em all!" I wasn't about to let anyone or anything beat me. This would be my "why!"

I decided to make it in life, despite not being supported by those that I felt should. When it was all said and done, I'd show them. I had no idea how, but I'd show them.

I spent my sophomore year of high school numb to the world, simply moving on autopilot. I jumped from my Uncle George's home to live in a hotel room, all while getting A's and Bs in school, even though I never studied I surrounded myself with my friends: Maurice, Liyongo, Marc, and Derrick. Somehow, I managed to keep my real life from them because I refused to let anyone pity me. I developed a way to mentally shut down any feelings or thoughts of what was happening to me by using my friends to make me laugh on the outside to keep me from dying on the inside. I guess you can say that I developed multiple personalities during that time since I was living two separate lives. I was Des to my classmates, Boobie to the streets, and never the two shall ever meet. I became their protector, and they became my family. Then, one day, I got a knock at my hotel room door from the angel that gave me the opportunity to begin the groundwork for a seven-year journey to partial healing.

"I don't care what you are doing; leave it all there and come with me!"

That angel's name was Susie Tolin (Gillam after marriage), and she just so happened to be my friend Liyongo's mother. I thought I'd never see her again after being ashamed of my recent actions of intervening in what was obviously an embarrassing matter while sleeping at their home during that past Thanksgiving.

I became a light sleeper since the incident at Reggie's house. So, I was quickly awakened by the commotion occurring in Susie's bedroom caused by her boyfriend, Donald Brown, his youngest sister's father, who was apparently upset with Susie about something. I woke Liyongo up because I felt he had the responsibility to protect his mother. Yet, Liyongo was not willing to intervene and asked that I just go back to sleep as well. Much to his surprise, I had already made up my mind that Donald had to get out of Susie's house, and I was gonna make sure he did!

They had no idea that I'd left my uncle's house because he would beat the crap out of his wife, and I didn't want to go to jail for killing him, especially since he was my mother's brother. Donald, on the other hand, was not family. I couldn't stand a man who even thought about beating women, which I truly believed might occur from the sound of his voice. That said, there was absolutely no way I was gonna let him put his hands on the woman who had treated me as though I were her own that entire Thanksgiving weekend. Like a man possessed, I burst into her bedroom to take matters into my own hands after Donald told me to stay in a boy's place. I immediately felt

I had somewhat betrayed her after Donald was put out of the house because she was never supposed to see that side of me. Anyway, when it was time to go, instead of Liyongo taking me home like he usually did, Susie told him to stay there, and she would drop me off. Though I can't remember what was discussed since I was embarrassed by my actions, she and I talked all the way to my destination. As we turned into the Northlander Inn, Susie looked at me in total disbelief, having absolutely no idea I lived in a motel room on 8 Mile Road.

"Is this where you live?"

The sound of her question actually shocked me because I figured Liyongo had told her since he had taken me home before, even though she had me give her directions while driving. I didn't want her to pry any further, so I told her that my mother lived there with me. I made up an excuse to make it seem as though we were in between places. Susie saw right through the lie and told me to go leave my mother a note that I would be living with her. She told me to leave everything I had in that room right where it was.

There she was in the parking lot of my motel, giving me a chance to get my life back on a positive course. So, without a thought, I did exactly what she said. I wrote a note to my mother and sat it on the dresser, knowing full well that no one would read it. I closed the door behind me as I followed her down the hallway, taking nothing. Susie took me into her home and called me her son from that very moment, treating me as though I had come out of her womb. To this very day, she introduces me to everybody she knows as her oldest son.

Though the Tolin home was now my home as well, my pride made me feel as though I was a burden. I operated as part of the family; yet, deep down, I didn't want to be there since subconsciously being there constantly reminded me that somebody knew my secret and "pitied" me. By the end of my junior year of high school, I had been accepted into multiple colleges. Still, I chose Michigan State University after receiving an on-the-spot admission to attend for the fall 1987-88 term. I knew I didn't want to live with the Tolins upon graduation from high school. I also knew full well that I had no idea how I was going to pay for college. One day, I walked into the Marine Corps Recruiters office in downtown Detroit and enlisted into the Marine Corps Reserves, ultimately being accepted into its delayed entry program since I had one more year of high school. According to my calculations, I would leave for boot camp a few days after graduation and finish Marine Corps Boot Camp a few weeks before the start of my freshman year at Michigan State. Though I was grateful for what Susie had done, I wanted to give my newly found family their lives back.

Susie was a single mother with three children of her own. Though we lived in a mansion, she inherited the home and the astronomical costs associated with the upkeep. I shared a room, clothes, and everything else with Liyongo. His two younger sisters had their own individual rooms, and Susie slept in the master, which was on the second floor of the home. There was a door halfway between Susie's and Semaja's bedroom that opened into a stairwell that would either take you into the kitchen or upstairs to the third floor, where there were another three or four bedrooms, a sitting room, and a full bath. The third floor was shut down during that time because no one ever went up there. I used to think my entire family could live on that third floor, especially considering it was larger than many places we had lived in the past. The easiest thing for me to have done would be to continue to live with the Tolins until whenever, but I owed it to Liyongo to give him his life back. I say that because everywhere he went, I had to go, including to his girlfriend's house, which is absolutely not ideal for a sixteen- or seventeen-year-old young man. I have to admit that, though I was finally safe, I felt trapped, as if I couldn't be me. My life, my existence, became intertwined with theirs. Though my thoughts had no merit, I felt as though I wasn't an individual at the Tolins'. I suppressed myself, making sure that I never expressed my feelings so as not to upset the household in any way, shape, or form. To me, I was not alive; I simply existed!

Enlisting into the Marine Corps Reserve was a "win-win" for me. The G.I. Bill would help me pay for college, and I wouldn't have to live with the Tolins after graduating high school. Though my plan seemed perfect on paper, I still had a few holes that I needed to fill:

- I was only seventeen, so I needed a parent's signature to enlist.

- Michigan State was expensive, so I needed to apply for financial aid, which also required my parents' financial information. I knew full well that the G.I. Bill wouldn't even put a dent in what I had to pay.

For some strange reason, I kept an old pay stub of my mother, which happened to have her SSN on it. Don't judge me, but I learned how to prepare taxes by using that information to forge the financial portion of the paperwork for college. I was awarded financial aid up to and including Pell Grants. As for my enlistment paperwork, my military records show:

Susie Gillium - mother

Father - deceased

As I said, I would show them!

## Collegiate Years

In September of 1987, I arrived on the campus of Michigan State University as an eighteen-year-old Marine with no study skills, multiple unresolved anger issues, and inner turmoil exacerbated by being surrounded by thousands of the very white people who I secretly hated. What made it worse was my newfound realization that the young collegiate women seemed to love me though they had no idea I had some serious mommy issues.

I spent my freshman year partying, drinking all the time, and making as many friends as I could to keep my mind off of my real life. I unconsciously reinvented myself and became known as the party guy. Though I had a girlfriend within the first few months on campus, I was sleeping with every woman who looked my way, including many of those who called themselves her friends. I didn't want to do it, but I couldn't stop. It was as though I were a drug addict, looking for his next fix. But once the act was done, I wanted absolutely nothing to do with the girl.

The truth was, I really liked my girlfriend. Still, since I couldn't trust a woman as far as I could spit in a hurricane, I didn't see the act as anything other than a release. I often had sex with someone else, especially when she and I had a disagreement. I found out that sex was a great stress reliever. Since women talk, one of them obviously put the word out that I knew what I was doing because the opportunities were endless. Most knew I was "seeing somebody," yet just acted like everything was normal whenever she was around. Women often simply gave me a sign that they wanted me to "stop by" when she was gone. I was in a "committed" relationship that was well known to all my peers while "hooking up" with multiple women whenever I felt the urge, and nobody seemed the wiser since my hook-ups remained silent.

According to Wikipedia, *Hookup culture* accepts and encourages casual sex encounters, including one-night stands and other related activities, without necessarily including emotional intimacy, bonding, or a committed relationship.

While the term *hookup* became commonly used in the 2000s, the 1980s, and the 1990s, encounters were equally, if not more prevalent, without the presence of social media causing problems. Campus life was crazy! Then, one day, everything went left.

I happened to have made it into my sophomore year after almost failing school as a freshman since I partied more than I attended any class. The only reason I got off academic probation was because my white academic counselor told me I should consider changing my major after reviewing my transcripts during a meeting. Since there was absolutely no way I was gonna ever let a white person believe that I was dumb, nor had I given her the authority to tell me what to do, I decided to prove her wrong by going to class every day. When grades were released, I had a 3.5 GPA that semester.

Anywho, one night, I was in my girlfriend's dormitory room relaxing during a party that was happening on her floor when her roommate decided she needed to confront me. She told me that she had just about enough of me constantly being in their room with my girlfriend, so I needed to get out and not come back. Her actions totally shocked me because I was one of the only people in our group who was incredibly nice to her, making sure she always had anything she needed. The only thing that I refused to do was sleep with her because she was both my girlfriend's roommate, as well as extremely unattractive. Though embarrassed by being put out, being the gentleman that I am, I told her that I was leaving. But I needed to say something before I went away.

I told her how confused I was by her putting me out since I was the only true friend she had, and I always treated her with honor and respect. Since all of that was now over because she had told me how she really felt, I explained that I could now tell her why everybody treated her different: "You are one of the ugliest women on the face of the earth, and that's why nobody wants to be around you!"

Feeling vindicated as laughter rang out all through the room, I turned around and strutted out of the door. My statement must have hit a nerve because her roommate ran behind me and punched me in the back of my head. When I regained consciousness, I was in the back of a campus police vehicle.

Instead of the punch knocking me out, it knocked me into the place where my suppressed rage took control. I was in the police car because she was sent to the hospital after I'd beaten the hell out of her, breaking her nose in the process. The only reason I didn't go to jail that night was because all the witnesses said I was walking away laughing when she ran behind me and attacked me while I had my back turned. Since I had every right to defend myself, the officers had no choice but to let me go.

Since it was a campus incident, the university had a trial to determine if I would be expelled. Yet, ultimately, it was determined that though expulsion was not justified, the damage to the other student created a situation where they had to do something. As it turns out, the university's actions were exactly what I needed. I was mandated to attend counseling, and Michigan State University paid for it.

Nobody but God would use an altercation like this to force a person hurting into seeing a professional to help deal with their internal demons. I would have never sought professional counseling. After all, I was too proud to seek help for myself because I believed I could figure it out by myself. That and the fact that I truly thought that needing help was a sign of weakness. This counseling turned out to be what I needed since, for the next few months, I had the opportunity to not only get things off my chest but also learn the foundational principles of the crisis management tactics necessary to lead me into living a productive life by controlling my anger.

For the first time, I became aware that my reaction to that particular incident was how I always reacted when I felt rejection. My actions took the form of anger; yet the anger was subconsciously a protection mechanism, used to keep me from feeling the hurt associated with a track record of rejection. It turned out that my outbursts of anger were my mind's way of keeping me from having a mental breakdown.

As a twenty-one-year-old young adult, I learned the 4 Cs of mental toughness:

1.  Confidence

2.  Control

3.  Commitment

4.  Challenge

These sessions made me feel alive again for the first time in a long time, and I looked forward to going. My newfound confidence overflowed into my campus life, so much so that I became outspoken concerning issues that the black students on campus were having after living a life where I was scared to look a man in the face because of Daddy. I was even elected as the President of the Wilson Hall Black Caucus. I began tutoring minority students in mathematics who lived in my dorm. I was well-known, well respected, and admired by many. I had a reputation for assisting whenever needed while bringing people together for the common good. That superhero that had been squashed deep down inside had risen once again.

In 1989, I even became head of security of the minority students' "Study In" on campus as we took over the administration building to bring awareness to how Black students were being treated on campus by both students and faculty alike. I felt purpose again, free, alive, and most of all, I felt safe. Then, as the end of the second term and the beginning of the summer season approached, I worried about how I would make it through the interim between summertime and the start of my junior year of college. During my final counseling session, I was given my direction:

"You are a great person, Des. But until you confront your mother about what she did, you will always struggle."

I couldn't explain it. But deep down, I knew he was telling me the truth. To move on and function as a productive member of society, I needed to have an adult conversation with my mother and ultimately forgive her—not for her sake—but for my own!

Toward the end of that school year, my girlfriend told me she was not coming back for our junior year. Instead, she transferred to Illinois State University to finish her degree at a less expensive school. She chose I-State because she was from Illinois and didn't have to pay out-of-state tuition. Since I was brand new to my healing process, and had not stopped my promiscuity as of yet, I knew there was no way I could deal with a long-distance relationship, even though I assured her we would be alright. I kept myself busy that summer because I went on active duty every summer for various training and spent time with my mother on occasions after our initial call when I literally cursed her out for abandoning me.

In her typical fashion, she turned it all on me by explaining her actions were due to the fact that I had (in her words) "become increasingly violent." Her explanation as to why she abandoned me was ultimately because she didn't want to stand by and watch me die. Though she never even acknowledged the white man, nor the trauma that I had experienced the entire time I lived with her, I decided to forgive her. I learned forgiveness is not for the person who has wronged you. It's for you so you can move on. To harbor unforgiveness actually gives the other person a sense of control over you. Once I understood that, I forgave people for just about everything. There was absolutely no way I was letting anybody control me.

By summer's end, I had a working relationship with my mother. I began the process to get her back into the lives of my brothers, whom I felt truly needed her more than me. My younger brothers now lived with Reggie after she had taken them to his house one day and never came back. My oldest brother had just been released from jail after taking the man who had accidentally shot through his house while shooting at a neighborhood friend. My middle brother was back and forth between Kalamazoo and Detroit, and all were in the "street pharmaceutical" business in one form or the other. My sister, on the other hand, had three children at that time and was living with their father. She ultimately married him after having four more kids by him, for a total of seven.

I'm not sure if it was my mother's pride or stubbornness that kept her from uniting with her children. Still, I often took her to one of their houses. Yet, she would refuse to get out of the car unless it was my sister's home. I was determined to get my family back together, so I kept trying.

I wanted us all to recognize that we all needed that lesson on forgiveness.

At the end of that summer, I returned to Michigan State University to begin my junior year of college on a mission to decompress from the stress of my family life. I knew full well that, if it were up to me, I would never have left campus. Campus life was indeed my safe space.

# Third Year of College

S ince my student loans, Pell Grant, work-study, and monthly checks from the military weren't nearly enough to cover room, board and tuition, I developed what I believe was a failsafe way to ensure I'd be able to stay in school:

Step 1: Register for fall classes.

Step 2: Use my second term Pell Grant to pay the previous balance so I could register for the second term.

Step 3: Save my earnings from my summer active duty to pay my second term balance and pay to enroll for the fall term.

After registering for the fall term of my third year, and my long-distance girlfriend breaking up with me because I told her about all the other women after she caught me, I decided to join a fraternity. I was ready to make a more significant impact in the community after seeing campus associates join. The person who offered me on-the-spot admissions turned out to be a member of mine.

I was preparing to apply to the College of Natural Science for my degree in Medical Technology. I couldn't do that until

I completed enough credits to be considered a junior. That's when I received a registered letter that informed me that on December 27, 1990, I was to report to Selfridge Air National Guard Base. I was officially being activated by the United States of America for Operation Desert Shield (Phase 1: Troop Build), which became Operation Desert Storm (Phase 2: Combat Phase - aerial and naval bombardment).

## Military Years

Since completing Marine Corps Boot Camp and coming home to attend college, it was a task for me to find a way to report to my duty station every month for weekend drill responsibilities because I couldn't afford school and a car. That was my reality of living in East Lansing, which was over 100 miles away from my duty station in Mount Clemens, Michigan. In 1987, I humbled myself and asked my Uncle George if I could use his house as a meeting place on the weekends. I had to report for duty. Sometimes, I had his wife take me to the base when I couldn't find a ride. I was blessed that one of the men who I was stationed with actually had a car and graduated high school with me, though we neither went to the same college nor hung out when we were in school. It just so happened that he saw me getting dropped off and picked up. He decided that we would link up every month to carpool; that way, one of us could drive his car while the other slept.

Jason White became my go-to person to ensure I showed up for duty. He became my "partner in crime" during our entire military career. Though we were in different platoons during boot camp, we did all of our remaining military training together. Everywhere I was stationed, Jason was right there. Boy, did he get us into trouble! That dude was my military 'ride or die.' But he absolutely could not hold his liquor. Jason, who was usually a 6'9" soft-spoken giant, turned into an absolute "butt hole" when he drank. He caused problems nearly everywhere we went, including one time we were coming from Tijuana, Mexico. There, he caused us to get into a fight with about twenty-five Hispanics after we crossed the border back into the U.S.!

Hanging out with him at the Non-Commission Officers (NCO) clubs on the bases (because that's where the women were) is what brought me to the conclusion that I would never get married while enlisted. Many of "those women" were the wives of soldiers who were either deployed or in the field for an extended period. Though the Articles of the Uniform Code of Military Justice (UCMJ) explicitly spelled out the punishment for adultery in the military, that place was an unadulterated cesspool, further solidifying my reason not to trust women. While I was grateful for the needed regime the Marine Corps was offering, as well as having the opportunity to travel and see other parts of the world, I absolutely wanted nothing to do with being enlisted long-term. It was lonely. I experienced firsthand what lonely people do.

None of us reservists wanted to be activated for Desert Storm, as many of us were college students. Yet, the Reserve units around the world were activated to man the bases stateside while the active-duty enlisted personnel were deployed as needed. My unit was one of the lucky ones, as Selfridge just happened to be at an Air Force Base. My Military Occupation Specialty (MOS) was 3534 (Contract Refuler). I refueled the very airplanes being used during the assault in Saudi Arabia. On my birthday, December 27, 1990, my unit was deployed to the desert training site in 29 Palms, which was the final training hub before deployment for the war.

I'm not complaining, but Operation Desert Storm lasted 43 days, from January 17 to February 28, 1991. However, my unit did not return home until June of 1991, which meant it was summertime. I had three months to keep myself out of trouble before I could get back to campus.

I had saved the majority of every paycheck from the war by sending it to this girl I was "messing around with" before I was activated. I had minimal expenses because the military fed, housed, and clothed me the entire time. I wanted personal savings outside of the military, so I sent it to her. I trusted neither my mother, who got a credit card in my name and ran it up, nor my uncle's wife, who had done the same after opening and using multiple credit cards that I had mailed to their address. Though I understood why my aunt did what she did, and I never held it against her, my mother was just blindly selfish. I knew I absolutely couldn't trust any family member to safeguard my savings.

When I returned from the war, it was summertime. School had already started, so all I had to do was hang out until the fall semester and complete my last two years of college. The first thing I did was go to an auction where I purchased my first car to eliminate my transportation issue. Then, I moved back into an off-campus apartment in East Lansing with my roommate, who I had when I got activated. Though I was no longer on the lease, he had no problem allowing me to move back in. The university allowed him to keep the apartment and only pay half the rent since they knew I only left because I was activated for the war. Derrick and I had been friends since high school. He saved 50% of the 50% he was paying, so my moving back in was a win/win for both of us, even though I wasn't taking classes.

Though I spent the first few months of that summer trying to catch up where I left off, I spent time in Detroit visiting my mother and brothers. My brother Pat had come to Detroit from Kalamazoo because he heard I was home from the war. While we were at my youngest brother's house one day, there was a family meeting called where all five of the boys were in attendance. For the first time in years, we were all in the same place, reminiscing about our common struggles and the importance of family. All of a sudden, the reason for the meeting was made clear. They wanted to go into the "street pharmaceutical" business as a family and needed money to get started. Since my life had been going in a different direction at that time, I let them know that I absolutely wanted *nothing* to do with it! As I looked around the room, however, my heart broke, knowing that my family was struggling. I had the power to help so, after a lengthy discussion, the five of us made an agreement that I would give them the money to purchase the initial drugs. They would pay me back off the top so I could go back to school in the fall. That decision sent my life into a downward educational spiral, taking years to recover.

A few days after the product was purchased and prepared, Liyongo asked me to go with him to a college party. So, I left my brothers and went to hang out with my friends. That night, I got 911 pages. I came back to the eastside that morning to find out that my brother Pat had shot and killed the man who was supposed to be the bodyguard of one of the neighborhood drug dealers. My younger brother Jamel and his running buddy Norman robbed this guy from time to time. Though it was Norman who actually continued to rob the guy, he never retaliated because he knew my brother Jamel was always with him. Jamel was considered untouchable because our oldest brother Joe's street name was ICE. He was actually the bodyguard for the man who supplied the drugs to all the dealers in that area. From what I was told, when they went to rob him as usual, his bodyguard showed them the gun in his waistband and informed them that all present and future plans were to stop. As usual, they came running to the family to let my brothers know what happened. When they told Pat about the gun he showed, he grabbed the sawed-off he brought with him from Kalamazoo. Though the young lady knew Norman, she only described Pat as the shooter to the police, not knowing he was a Pennington since he spent most of his time in Kalamazoo. With Pat being on the run from the police, my youngest brother Dwight stole the money and all the drugs that had been purchased for the "family business," which meant I wouldn't be able to register for fall classes. Though I wanted to kill my brother for what he had done, my blind loyalty to my family led me to take Pat out in East Lansing with me until things blew over.

Pat and I spent the rest of that summer partying with my collegiate friends and even went to Jones Beach in New York for their Greek Picnic. I introduced the Sigma All Male Review to the campus that I was a participant in while on leave in 29 Palms California at the University of California State

Northridge, which was nothing more than a strip show for collegiate women where they paid us for our entertainment.

All of my college friends loved my brother as much as they did me after I had him perform at one of the shows, though no one knew why he had all of a sudden been everywhere I was. Then, one day, those who read the paper found out that he was Detroit's most wanted after a newspaper article was published with his face and the story. Though I immediately took him to his best friend Micheal Easter's apartment to get him away from my college friends and informed my core group about why I really had him there, when classes began, my roommate moved out because he had already gotten into some legal trouble with the university and his father happened to be a sergeant in the Detroit Police Department. Since I was neither on the lease, nor a student, I found a job as a security guard. I moved into an off-campus apartment with two female roommates, attempting to save money to get back into school.

None of my fraternity brothers knew I wasn't in school because, when I wasn't working, I was always on campus and still attended every meeting. We continued partying every weekend, often going on road trips from campus to campus throughout Michigan and Ohio. I became pretty popular, and my frat brothers always saw me with a different woman. I tried to make sure I had somewhere to lay my head if we got too drunk, no matter where we went. One weekend, we came to a house party in Ypsilanti, and I laid eyes on a young lady I realized I'd seen no matter what party we attended. As a matter of fact, she was always with this girl named Felicia (Fee), whom I knew from Eastern Michigan University as one of the Sigma Sweethearts. Since my regular "hookup" wasn't there, I whispered to my boy who rode with me that I was going to add the new girl to my list for the night. As soon as I was done with my sentence, he ran up to her and danced with her all night, never allowing me to get a word in. The truth of the matter was that I was hotter than fish grease, though I refused to let him know. He even had the nerve to brag about dancing with the prettiest girl in the room all night, even though he wasn't even interested in her.

That following weekend, I saw her at a party at Oakland University. Though I already had a regular "hookup" there, I made it a point to make a move on her and asked her to dance. Though I was sweating profusely from strolling around the party with my frat brothers, when a slow song came on, she didn't push me away as I reached for her hand. By the end of the night, I knew her name was Nicole. She had attended Wilberforce University and was currently working at Blue Cross Blue Shield. I thanked her for the dance and for not pushing me away, and I went to find my Oakland hookup. When I saw Nicole at Eastern Michigan the following weekend, I not only danced with her for the majority of the evening, but I also asked her for her telephone number after announcing, "You might as well give me your number since I see you every weekend!"

Though she told me that was a bad pick-up line, she still gave me the number, even though I never used it. I didn't call it because the truth was I actually added it to the rotation of the women I would call when I wanted company. Since she was new, she was at the bottom of the list. Two weeks later, I saw her at the party that weekend and realized that she hadn't been to the prior two parties. Instantly, I decided to use her absence as a means of a pickup line to avert the question as to why I had not called. When our eyes met, I walked straight up to her as if I were mad and said, "Why did you give me the wrong number? I've been looking for you for two weeks!" It turned out that the phone line she shared with her uncle at her grandmother's house was cut off because he didn't pay the bill, even though she had given him her half. Then she went on to explain that she had missed the last two weeks because her grandfather on her father's side had passed away, so she'd been in New Jersey. I felt like crap for my approach, but I spent the rest of the evening keeping her company because I could tell she was still mourning her grandpa. At the end of the evening, she gave me her new number, explaining that it was hers alone and that it wouldn't get disconnected.

I called Nicole every night from that day on. We talked for hours. We'd lay on the phone, learning what each other felt were the important things in life, such as family, finances, and friendships. We often laughed at one another's stories concerning how people thought they were getting over on us in past relationships. We talked about what we would and would not put up with. Then, at the end of the conversation, I would ask her to let me take her out on a date. She always declined. I'd humorously end our conversation with, "Well, I'll talk with you tomorrow!" and then hang up.

Everybody who knew her knew full well that Nicole had one rule, which she told me from day one: "I don't date Sigmas!" Especially those like me who had a plethora of women because I was a collegiate stripper that she had seen in action.

Though she knew of my reputation when we saw each other at parties on the weekends, we'd give each other the biggest hugs and make sure that we spent a little time talking or dancing before going our separate ways. I'd always call her that night to make sure she had made it home safely. One day, I noticed something; I hadn't hooked up with another girl in quite some time, and the truth was that

I had no desire to do so. I tried to snap out of it and go back to hooking up, but all I could think about was Nicole. That's when my nightly requests to take her out became real. I realized that I was at peace and could be vulnerable with her. She wanted nothing from me other than my personal friendship. Finally, one night, Nicole said, "Yes!"

## Nicole Boyd

After at least an hour-long conversation, I ended our call with the now-evolved statement: "I'll be in Detroit for the weekend. Can I take you out?" She said yes, but I hung up the phone.

Seconds later, I realized what she said, and I called her back. I got an earful of how full of it I was, just like everybody else. I quickly calmed her down after explaining that I actually wouldn't be able to take her out because I had to report to Selfridge Air National Guard Base for my monthly military duties. I convinced her, however, to allow me to come to her house to spend a little time with her on my way to report for duty.

With the excitement of a teenager, I pulled up to her house. I proudly rushed to the door and was she introduced me to her grandmother, grandfather, and, later, her mother, who had stopped by. Though we all had a great conversation, her grandfather and I really hit it off. I had no idea that he didn't like any of the male friends and/or husbands of his family. He often went to his bedroom and closed the door anytime one of them came to visit. Leon Bacon, Jr. and I found out that we had many things in common. We graduated from the same prestigious Detroit high school, Cass Technical High School. We were also both military men, although he was in the Army. He and I sat in his den all night discussing life and family. I was so excited that Nicole said I could come over that I locked my keys in my car. I was totally embarrassed because I had to spend the night when no one could get the door open. At about 5 a.m. the next morning, Nicole's family watched as the military police opened my car door and took me to the base because I was AWOL. None of that mattered to me because *she had said yes*!

Though it was quite some time before we actually told any of our friends, Nicole and I have been a couple ever since that, *yes*! In fact, I asked Nicole to marry me four months after her *yes* in October, and she became my wife the following year on June 19, 1993.

I was now a twenty-four-year-old husband with a twenty-two-year-old wife. I was also in a world of trouble because neither one of us had any idea what the hell we were doing. In fact, I often asked her to forgive me, and I reminded her, "I'm just making this up as I go along."

# Building a Family

## Young and in Love

*"Being deeply loved by someone gives you strength, while loving someone deeply gives you courage."*
–LAO TZU

Statistics show that in 1993, the median age of marriage in the United States was 26.5 for men and 24.5 for women. Ironically, this has increased over time, as in 2023, the median for men grew to 30.2 and 28.4 for women. In addition, the divorce rate (number of divorces per 1,000 married women) was 21 per 1,000 in 1993. What's even more interesting is that the divorce rate for our age bracket at that time was the highest among all at 47 per 1,000. Though we had no idea of the statistics, the truth was all signs indicated that she and I were not gonna make it!

For your consideration, here are the top reasons given for divorce:

1. Lack of commitment - 75%

2. Infidelity- 59.6%

3. Conflict and arguing - 57.7%

4. Marrying too young - 45.1%

5. Financial problems - 36.7%

6. Substance abuse - 34.6%

7. Domestic violence - 23.5%

8. Feeling underappreciated or neglected, jealousy and sexual rejection rounded off the list of the top ten at minimal percentages.

Our foundation was formed around the multiple discussions she and I had concerning the top two before her yes. Still, the rest of the reasons for divorce were identified while we were hitting full throttle. As a young couple, we had made a pact centered around three things:

- 100% commitment to each other

- Never allow anyone to come between us

- Never go to bed angry (we had many sleepless nights!)

Nobody outside our tiny one-bedroom apartment knew that our immaturity caused us to be in constant conflict and that we fought like cats and dogs. I was an uncontrollable mental midget due to the untapped emotional baggage I possessed. I had no idea what a husband was. I was quite frankly scared to death. So, I yelled all the time, masquerading as an alpha male hell-bent on running a household, and Nicole wasn't having it. She may have been the most angelic being I ever laid eyes on, but her beauty covered imprints of her own that sent her into attack mode at the slightest sense of anything that resembled what she experienced when her mother and father were married. She had never given a single hint while we were dating, so how was I supposed to know that raising my voice would eventually cause her to attack me?

I never retaliated in kind to her attacks because she wasn't as big as a fly, and her attacks could never hurt me. Yet, I was totally convinced she needed to see somebody before I lost it. Every now and then, I'd shake her around like a rag doll in hopes that she'd snap out of her rage, and we'd laugh about her actions when she came back to herself. We were broke. She was crazy. I was a mental case, and we were madly in love with each other. Nicole and I were two imperfect people, but absolutely perfect for each other.

Then, one day, I had just about enough. She had become visibly upset with me for some reason because my baby brother (who happens to be a Muslim) said she had no say in where we would be eating during a discussion after a rehearsal for his wedding. Though I immediately told him we weren't going where he wanted, and that my wife wasn't his wife, unbeknownst to me, she got upset with me anyway. After a long period of silence, as I was driving us home, like a mad person, Nicole attacked me out of nowhere. She slapped me in the back of my head and punched me in the shoulder. It took everything in me to keep us from running into a wall on the freeway. When she attacked again as we walked into our apartment, I violently threw her across the room. I grabbed my keys and went for a drive to keep myself from putting my hands on her. I had promised myself that I would never hit the woman I loved, but she had pushed me to my breaking point.

I drove to a park near our apartment. As I sat in the car, I took off my wedding ring, furious because I knew I was powerless to stop myself from what I would do if I went back to that apartment if she attacked me again. After about thirty minutes of sitting in the car, trying to calm down, I began to weep as I realized that, for the first time in my life, I had someone who was madly in love with me. Though I loved her equally, I was unable to understand or prohibit the triggers that had us at each other's throats. Nicole opened my eyes to a place where I could see true beauty in the world again. She introduced me to safety through her love, which I had longed for all of my life.

I couldn't understand why we fought so much, why our love wasn't enough, and, more importantly, why I was scared to go home. Before I knew it, I was crying uncontrollably while banging on my steering wheel and yelling at the top of my lungs. *Why? Why! Why?* As clear as day, I heard, "If you would send me someone who would love me for me, I'll serve you for the rest of my life!"

I was sitting alone in a parked car with no one else around me. I thought, *Who said that?! Because it sure wasn't me!*

I clearly heard the very words that I had uttered most of my life. Only this time, they hadn't come out of my mouth! Then, all of a sudden, for the first time in my life, I felt an overwhelming presence of peace that I cannot explain even to this day. I don't know how, but I clearly understood that it was the voice of God telling me that I was not fulfilling my end of the bargain. Wiping the tears from my eyes and blowing my nose to get my composure, I returned my wedding ring to its rightful place. I drove back to our apartment as a brand-new man with a new perspective on life.

I would spend the rest of my life as an imperfect man, searching for the truth in God, serving Him as He taught me through His Word how to be a husband, father, and brother … and how to live a victorious life as a godly Christian man. After hearing the voice of God speaking to me, I was never the same.

# Living a Christian Life

I was ordained to preach the Gospel at the Agape Temple Bible Training Institute on October 19, 1995. I'd spent the previous two years totally committed to understanding the mysteries of the Scripture, religion, and learning who God truly was. I offered a unique perspective as I served the Christian community, having not been indoctrinated with "*churchism*" as I didn't grow up in it. I had a burning desire to understand and teach the Scriptures based on what was on the mind of God. From the moment I dedicated my life to the Lord, I spent most of my free time studying His Word and spending time in prayer with Him. I felt as if I owed that to God and needed to make up for the lost time. Though remaining cordial, I stopped most communication with the people who reminded me of my former life. I committed myself to the things of God, Nicole, and my new church family.

Nicole and I had become foster parents four months into our marriage after taking my sister's youngest two boys into our home due to them going into the system from abuse. We really wanted children of our own and had multiple discussions even before we were married. Still, we were childless, though actively trying since day one. She and I had made an agreement early on that when she got pregnant, whoever was making the most money would continue to work while the other stayed home to raise our children. We came to that agreement knowing that she made twice as much money as I did and carried insurance for both of us through her job. I was all in, however, because having a parent at home was extremely important to me based on how I was raised. Nicole was onboard because that's what she saw as she lived with her grandparents after her parents' divorce. She and I were in total agreement that we both wanted two or three boys, which made us wonder if God had answered our prayers through my nephews living with us in our two-bedroom apartment. That is until the decision was made that it was best for them to return the system to be reunited with my sister and her husband with their five other children.

One night, as I slept peacefully, I vividly recall a dream that I would share for the next seven years, which can be heard in multiple taped sermons I gave while delivering the Word of God across Metro Detroit from 1993 to 2000.

I dreamed of casually strolling hand in hand near the beach, admiring the peacefulness of the day, enjoying the wind and my company. After some time, I noticed that the hand I was holding was much smaller than Nicole's. I looked down and saw the face of an angel looking up at me, grinning from ear to ear. As I looked into those eyes, I felt a peace that I had only experienced through my wife's eyes. I noted the hair and complexion that Nicole carried and then heard the words, "*Hi, Daddy; my name is Destiny!*"

I woke up with tears flowing down my face, praising God for the vision of a little girl named Destiny, who called me her daddy. There was no doubt in my mind that God had just shown me that He had heard our petition and promised us a child whose name was to be Destiny. When my wife woke to console me, believing I was sad about something, I shared my dream and asked her to stand with me, believing that Destiny was on her way. We both were excited that we would have a child, even though it wouldn't be a boy.

For the next seven years, I testified about God's promise of our baby girl Destiny. We even purchased baby clothes from time to time, which we stored in a crate in the room of the first home we purchased. We would sometimes sit in Destiny's room thinking about how we longed to have her be in her room, especially when Nicole's cycle came around because it indicated that she was not pregnant yet. By 1999, we were doing well financially because Nicole had been with the same company for ten years. I was not only in ministry, but also a million-dollar producing realtor who happened to be a full-time employee in the auto industry.

I had become a workaholic, dividing my time between the plant and my real estate office and preparing for Sunday morning services, including the weekly class I taught at 9:30 a.m. Nicole and I began a marriage ministry that we called One Flesh, which became a community of believers dedicated to the marriage covenant. It also provided a safe place to learn and grow as individual couples.

One day, one of the newly married women asked Nicole to sit with her for a counseling session after church. A few hours later, Nicole came home furious, crying uncontrollably after meeting with the young lady. She screamed at the top of her lungs, "I told that lady to go find somebody else because there was no way I could counsel her!"

It appeared that this newlywed, who was not more than one year into marriage, was pregnant and that it wasn't her husband's baby! Nicole was ranting through the house, complaining about how she was living a faithful life to both God and her husband. Yet, somebody cheating on her husband got pregnant and not her; I grabbed her by the arms, pulled her close to me, and told her to stop. While looking into her tear-filled eyes, preparing to give her words of encouragement like I always did, I opened my mouth and said, "Baby, you are pregnant! God says don't worry; it's your time. You are pregnant!"

Though Nicole stared at me through watery eyes, calmed and surprised by my declaration, she placidly asked that I not play with her like that. I, too, was shocked by the words that so loosely flowed from my lips. Yet, for some strange reason, I was utterly convinced that what had been uttered was as true as my name itself! As I jumped with excitement, grabbing Nicole's hands and then rushing to the drug store to buy a pregnancy test, praising God all the way, I emphatically continued to demand that my wife stand in agreement with me.

When we returned with our purchase, I had her take a test in our main bathroom. Upon being engulfed in screams of exhilaration from the results, I had her immediately go to the basement bathroom to take another test explaining the Scripture in Deuteronomy 19:15:

> *"...at the mouth of two witnesses, or at the mouth of three witnesses, shall the matter be established."*

God had given me a Word of knowledge concerning my wife, which was proven through the pregnancy tests and manifested nine months later with the birth of Destiny Joy Pennington, the little girl I saw in my dream nearly eight years prior to her birth.

Seeing Destiny's face as she entered the world through the birth canal and looked into my eyes instantly humbled me and gave me an overwhelming sense of purpose. I openly wept from the understanding that I was now responsible for a life while struggling to understand how anyone could neglect such a task. Her birth invigorated me to both remember and react to unfulfilled dreams. Those dreams would position my life to a place ensuring I'd be in a position to take care of the tremendous responsibility of fatherhood that I had been given.

Two weeks after Nicole returned to work from maternity leave, she put in her resignation to become a full-time homemaker, choosing her family over her career as I re-enrolled in college and conferred my BA in Business Management. This accomplishment led to being promoted to supervisor at a company that I would ultimately retire from after nearly three decades of various positions with increasing responsibilities.

Finally, we began to operate as a complete family. Nicole had wholeheartedly embraced her role as the "manager" of the Pennington household, of which I enthusiastically was the financial provider for the two people I loved the most. I was Nicole's husband and Destiny's father, living an abundant life filled with extreme thankfulness to God for honoring our request to operate as a one-income household.

Yet, I was missing something.

# Reconciliation

*"Reconciliation and forgiveness can actually help all of us move on in a healthier, happier way."*
–CHESA BOUDIN

## Filling in the blanks

Nicole grew up with a maternal family who did just about everything together. They seemed to enjoy each other's company so much that they had family reunions nearly every summer in different states where hundreds of members showed up each year. Our lives were completely intertwined with her family and extended family, including in the church where we worshiped since her uncle was the pastor. I must admit, at the beginning of our relationship, I struggled with the concept of an extended family that actually communicated with each other, enjoying spending time together, having never experienced it before. I actually thought it was utter madness that they were always around. I even expressed my discomfort with my wife from time to time. I often felt out of place; yet, I made sure to participate in her family events when asked simply because I knew it made her happy.

The birth of my daughter reminded me that I, too, had an extended family, which birthed in me an internal desire for reconciliation, realizing that Destiny deserved to know both sides of her bloodline. Though my oldest brother started checking up on Nicole when she was pregnant, and my mother and younger brother Jamel met Destiny when I attended his wedding in Florida three months after she was born, I made my rounds to introduce the rest of my family to Destiny shortly after our Florida trip.

My Uncle George was the only real family member on my maternal side living in Detroit whose residence was known to me. So, I made it a point to spend time with my Aunt Sharleen, his wife, to use as a catalyst in finding contact information concerning my maternal family. I went through Aunt Sharleen because neither mom nor her brother was willing to discuss the topic since they couldn't care less about any of their family members and, for some strange reason, up to and including each other.

Atlanta became our newest vacation spot after finding out my granddad had relocated there after retirement. During my visits, I'd spend time sitting at his feet, in awe of who he was to me as he poured out his heart concerning the importance of life, faith, and family. He shared stories of the history of the Wadleys, including the painful memories of the extreme racism he experienced as a young man that ultimately drove him to leave his wife and children in the south and migrate north. He spoke openly about his love for my grandmother Louise and, more importantly, how her death affected Momma so much that she was placed in a mental institution for a short time after attacking Granddad. He recalled Momma's childhood and the toxic marriage she and Daddy had, where Daddy would leave every time she got pregnant, professing the baby she carried wasn't his. From what I gathered, Grandma Louise's best friend was a lady I knew as my Aunt Mabel. She and Aunt Mabel raised their children together. So, just like in the tradition of every African American family, they were considered cousins. It appeared that when Daddy would leave during Momma's pregnancies, her "cousin" would always come to her aid to assist her as she navigated through the birthing process. But here's the kicker: Her "cousin's" name was Desmond Moore!

Momma's and Desmond's unapproved relationship is what ultimately ostracized her from the family because, not only did they have two children together, but I also found out years later that Dez was already married with two young boys of his own. Aunt Mabel, Granddaddy, and every other member of my maternal adult family knew what was happening. Yet, they chose to distance themselves from Momma and her children and never tell Desmond's wife.

The sad thing is Jamel and Dwight never even met their older brothers. Nor did they have any contact with their father since, shortly after the machete incident happened, they were less than eight years old.

Grandma Louise never knew of their relationship because she died before I was born after choosing to use the services of a "faith healer" instead of a certified physician when she became ill. According to Granddaddy, Momma blamed him for her mother's death because he was always working and didn't make her go to the doctor. This, according to Granddaddy, is why Momma attacked him and landed in a mental institution.

As my grandfather poured out his heart to me through the many conversations we had, I couldn't help but reach the conclusion one day that I was the son of a woman with unmedicated mental issues, doing the best she could to fit into a society that rejected and shunned her.

Unfortunately, it was a rejection that she ultimately passed down to her children. I can only surmise that she was hell-bent on showing everybody that she didn't need them and allowed her pride to isolate her children from their extended family, even though we desperately needed help. This revelation made me understand the foundational upbringing of my life, which led me to see my mother through the eyes of compassion for her own struggles.

During one of my final trips to visit Granddad right before he was placed in hospice, I couldn't help but notice Granddad was surrounded by the love of a devoted wife while being adored by his baby girl, Nicole, her four daughters, and their families. One day, when we were alone talking, he shared his inner sadness concerning the fact that he had six other natural children with families who never came around. Granddad was evidently heartbroken because he wept as he shared his longing to also be surrounded by his own offspring to share in his life. While my Aunt Flora would call from time to time, he had not spoken to my Uncle George in decades. He had neither seen nor spoken to my mother since we left Kalamazoo when we were children. I was so moved by his sadness that I called my mother. When she answered, I gave the phone to my Granddaddy without telling her I was sitting at her father's bedside. After they talked for about ten minutes, he gave me back the phone. I ended the call not caring; yet, knowing full well Momma was pissed. I did the same thing a little later by calling my Uncle George's house because I determined they would both have to just get over it. Their father was nearly ninety years old and deserved to hear from them from time to time, no matter what their issue may have been. I even brought my oldest brother Joe and his girlfriend with me one year so he could spend time with more of his grandchildren.

Sadly, my grandfather died two years after the birth of Destiny. Though I was heartbroken, I was honored to know that he got to hold his great-granddaughter and left this world with the full knowledge that he was both loved and adored by his entire family. Though Momma didn't attend the funeral, the rest of his living children were there, including Uncle George, Aunt Flora, and, of course, my Aunt Nicole. During the repast, I made sure that I introduced myself to everyone as one of Loretta's kids. I exchanged information with the family members who were the offspring of his younger sister, who lived in Illinois and whom I never knew existed. My newfound family was shocked to hear about Loretta's children, and the elders seemed uneasy as I mentioned her name and shared how we were doing:

- Rosa married her long-time boyfriend, Kenneth Mathes, and they had seven children together.

- Joseph, Jr. had been married, divorced, and had three children.

- Petris had two children and resided in Michigan (though I did not share that his actual residence was in a Michigan Correctional Facility as an inmate at that time).

- I was a successful businessman and pastor, married with one child.

- Jamel was married and living in Florida. He and his wife were in a blended family of five children, two of whom were his biological children, though they treated them all the same.

- Dwight was in his second marriage and living in Michigan. He had seven children between three women.

Though Momma wasn't there, I wanted each of them to know that she and her children were just fine. While driving my family back to Detroit from the funeral, as they slept, I wept from an overwhelming revelation that I would leave this life, having never known my extended family. I could have possibly suffered from a secret loneliness like Granddad if I weren't actively working to break that cycle. This revelation motivated me even more to satisfy my longing to reconcile with my extended family. It was my job to fix what they had broken, not for me, but for Destiny. Now that I had connected with my maternal side, it was time for me to find my father's people. Even though I knew Daddy hated me, and though I was a preacher of the Gospel, I hated him even more.

# My Father's People

"Daddy's" brother (Uncle Austin Williams) gave me his address in Ypsilanti on Jeff Street years ago by my Uncle Austin one day, who happened to be Daddy's younger brother. My oldest brother Joe had always stayed connected with Uncle Austin because they both worked out all the time and had the physique of bodybuilders. Uncle Austin didn't mainly deal with his older and only brother because he couldn't understand why he refused to raise his boys, so he often referred to him as "that selfish S.O.B." Though neither attended my wedding, he had finally given me the address so Nicole and I could invite Daddy to our nuptials. Since we never received a *"Return to Sender,"* indicating it was incorrect, I always assumed it had reached him, and he just decided not to attend. Nicole and I built a relationship with Uncle Austin's family, and we remained in communication with his wife even after he died.

One day, Nicole and I were invited to a birthday party in Ypsilanti by our friend Shanta Langford. As our children played, I struck up a conversation with her, eventually telling her that my father lived in Ypsilanti on Jeff Street. Since I knew that the city of Ypsilanti wasn't as big as Detroit, and I was aware she grew up there, I asked if she knew where the street was. Though she was confident of having no recollection of a street bearing that name, while I was placing the baby in the car in preparation to leave, I read the street sign of the crosswalk directly outside her door. I was flabbergasted that it was the very Jeff Street that I had asked her about during our conversation! The very next weekend, I located the address Uncle Austin gave me.

I packed my family in our car for a family drive. After stopping by our friend's house for a quick laugh and telling her she needed to be more aware of her surroundings since Jeff Street was right outside her door, I drove to the address. I knocked on the door, not knowing what to expect next.

Much to my surprise, Daddy answered the door and said something that I had never heard come out of his mouth in all my life.

"Des?!"

His utterance of my name totally took me by surprise as I was now a thirty-two-year-old man. However, it was the first time I heard my name come out of his mouth! Collecting myself, I explained that I was married with a young child, and I wanted him to meet my family that were currently sitting in my car.

It turned out that Daddy was on his third wife, Deborah, and had a daughter, Jovanna, who was just a toddler, a little older than Destiny. Pushing through the internal damage from the years of abuse and neglect at his hands, I further swallowed my pride, ignoring the anger that was bubbling inside and realizing I needed this forgiveness for my family's sake. Over the next year, I further humbled myself. I developed an open line of communication with him and his new family both for Destiny's benefit. Because the disdain in his eyes for me was no longer present, especially after he found out how successful I was both as a realtor and manager in my company. I even took my oldest brother to see him one day after I shared with the rest of my siblings that I had found Daddy and his new family. The only thing we could agree on concerning Daddy was they all wanted absolutely nothing to do with him.

I was surprised one day when Joe asked me to take him to see him out of the blue, and I eagerly complied. Unbeknownst to me until later, Joe's plan was to beat the hell out of him on sight, but he was moved with compassion when he noticed how small and frail Daddy was when he saw him. Deborah was stern, yet much younger than Daddy. She had met him during the time they worked as correctional officers at the Women's Huron Valley Correctional Facility, where he retired. On one of our visits, she shared with me her plans to join him in retirement soon. However, I could hardly concentrate as my eyes were fixed on him, thinking about what he used to do to my older sister as Jovanna sat on his lap. I learned it was time to end a visit anytime I felt anger bubbling up inside of me. I often left because he was so evasive when it came to discussing his extended family with me every time I tried to have the conversation, which made me more determined to find my father's relatives.

Within the next two years, I relocated to Illinois to manage in another capacity within my company, which made my periodic stops at his home far less frequent. I continued to call him from time to time, however, even though it was apparent that our relationship was one-sided since the only time we talked was when I reached out to check up on him. Though they had relocated to Georgia after Deborah's retirement, she and I made an agreement that she would contact me if anything happened to him. I confided in her about my distress in finding out his mother had died from one of my friends three years after her transition when he found out that I was related to the owner of the video game we were playing at our local store. Most of the video games in Metro Detroit displayed the King and Williams Music moniker on the side. Trying to show off, I explained that Mr. Williams was actually my daddy's stepfather, which made him my grandpa. My distress came when he said to me, "I was so sad when Ms. Lillian died; I really liked her!"

Mr. Williams married Lillian and began raising Daddy at an early age, a few years before she gave birth to my Uncle Austin. He was a successful businessman who, among other things, owned the neighborhood record store, employing many of the youth back in the day, including my mother. I knew him well because I made it a point to stop by his record store to spend time with him all the time after my oldest brother Joe took me to his shop one day when I was in ninth grade and told me who he was. Though he and Lillian had divorced when I was small, he treated me like I was his grandson. He proudly displayed pictures and accolades of me on the walls of his shop. I shared every accomplishment with him through the years, partially hoping that he would tell Daddy, who would finally come looking for me and tell me how proud he was of me. Pictures of my high school graduation, me wearing my Marine Corps dress blues, and copies of my many academic accomplishments served as wallpaper in that shop. Though he died before Destiny was born, I had a chance to introduce him to Nicole and have pictures of us together, as he was the only person from that side who attended our wedding.

Now that I had somewhat reconciled with Daddy, Deborah and I had an agreement that she would not let me find out that he died from anybody else but her. Though we still had a somewhat awkwardly distant relationship, I made sure that I stayed connected with them to keep them abreast of how Daddy's other children and grandchildren were doing, especially considering my siblings' open expressions of disdain for him. While I had convinced myself that my contact with my parents through the years was to ensure I could move forward, and that they knew their grandchildren, there was an uncontrollable motivation deep within, which I realized that I may have been keeping them around to show them that what they had thrown away excelled beyond imagination.

I was, by far, the most successful person on either side of the family, making significant decisions in a Fortune 500 company, owning a 3700 square-foot home that we built, and pastoring a church that I planted in Rockford, Illinois. Life was good!

Yet, somehow, it still felt incomplete.

# The Revelation of Me

*"The heart of a father is the masterpiece of nature."*
–ANTOINE-FRANCOIS

F atherhood is about so much more than being a father, encompassing the love, support, guidance, and protection a man provides to his children. It also involves nurturing, teaching, and shaping of the lives of his offspring through positive role modeling and active involvement in a child's upbringing. It's about being present, dependable, and emotionally connected, fostering a strong bond and sense of security. It requires patience, sacrifice, and dedication to instill values, morals, and life skills that will help children grow into confident, responsible, and well-rounded individuals.

A young man growing up without a father can, therefore, face a range of potential risks, including difficulties with forming healthy relationships, struggles with self-esteem, increased likelihood of behavioral problems, lower academic achievement, higher risk of substance abuse, and challenges with identity development due to a lack of a positive male role model to guide them through life stages and social norms associated with masculinity.

My brothers and I were now adults with children of our own, attempting to navigate this thing called fatherhood through a definition of masculinity borne from the survival mentality we were forced into. The one thing we each agreed on, without ever having a conversation, is that we would be present in our children's lives—no matter what.

*"The two most important days in your life are the day you are born, and the day you figure out why."*
–MARK TWAIN

The one thing that life has taught me, which I have humbly shared with many, is that everything you do today will affect you for the rest of your life.

If there was anything I wish someone had told me when I was making my transition from high school into manhood, it would be that everything in your life has purpose. I encourage those with an ear to hear. You already have everything inside of you to ensure a successful future. It is up to you, however, to take the steps necessary to become who you were created to be.

I once sent the following encouraging message to a young man named Noah, whom I mentored. He had graduated from high school and was on his way to college. I asked him to place these words on the door of his dorm room so he could see them on his way out: Noah,

- You have been dedicated to God and will forever be surrounded by His people who are a family outside of your family. *Put God 1st in everything you do.*

- Your quiet and reserved demeanor is a perfect foundational gift for success because it gives you the time necessary to analyze any situation. Learn to use that gift. *Always take your time, and don't stop watching.*

- You have proven to yourself and others that you are able to accomplish anything you set your mind to do. *Believe in yourself and never give up.*

I realized that my life experiences were actually a gift that brought hope to many when shared, especially during times of trouble. In spite of my beginning, God had chosen to bless me beyond my wildest dreams, and I showed my thankfulness by sharing my time, talent, and treasures in every area of my life. By the time I reached the age of forty-five, Nicole and I had relocated back to Michigan and had three beautiful children. I was preaching the Gospel, flourishing in a rewarding career, surrounded by people who loved me … until I received a call from my brother Jamel on March 3, 2016. Our mother had died!

Though I had eulogized many in my twenty-three years of ministry at that time, my mother's eulogy was the most difficult panegyric I have ever given. I was inundated with the unfortunate things that occurred at the hands of my youngest brother Dwight in the last months before her transition. Momma lived to be seventy-two and had six children (the five married were to people she didn't like for no reason at all), twenty-four grandchildren, and thirteen great-grandchildren. Though I was at peace with our relationship, and she had expressed on numerous occasions how proud she was of the family man I had become, losing her affected me in a way that is best explained as a hole in the heart that can never be filled.

Five months prior to her transition, I took my family to visit her at the Sable Palm HealthCare Center of Largo, Florida, after finding out Dwight had placed her in the facility and moved his family from Michigan into her home. Though I flew Momma out to stay with us for the summer when we lived in Illinois, I had not seen her for two years during the time my company relocated me back to Michigan. Nicole gave birth to Joshua in March of 2013 and Lauryn in December 2014. Momma was blind at the time as a result of diabetes but had a chance to hold and kiss her youngest two grandchildren, whom she was meeting for the first time. When Momma died, I went on an emotional roller coaster.

- **Extreme Anger** - Though Jamel had informed me on Tuesday, March 3, Momma actually died on Sunday, March 1. Dwight was on record at the center as her contact person, and he came to see her when she died and walked out after his visit, never telling any of us. Momma's body lay in that room for two days before the center found a contact number for Jamel. From Michigan, I arranged to have her body picked up and flown to Florida for her funeral, paying for everything. Though Momma had life insurance, Dwight had power of attorney, and no one could find him, including his wife and children, who were living in Momma's house. It turned out that he had not only cashed in on her insurance policy, but he also had her sign a quitclaim deed to her house to him before placing her in the center. It took me six years to go knock on his door and tell him I forgive him for what he did, though the rest of the family has neither seen him nor have a desire to.

- **Depression** - After the funeral, anytime I thought about her, I'd weep while struggling to understand why I couldn't control it. Momma hadn't been a major part of my life since she abandoned me. Still, after our reconciliation, I always made sure to at least call her from time to time just to say hello. Not being able to at least call her was not the source of depression, however. I had her body cremated before arriving in Florida, so I never saw her deceased remains. Instead, my last memory of Momma is a photo of her kissing her granddaughter Lauryn, as I held her when we visited Momma in October. So, this was not the source either. After a few years, I determined that the depression came from a deep sadness that she died alone, misunderstood, and taken advantage of by someone she gave birth to, and there was nothing I could do about it. Sadly, not more than twenty people attended her funeral. Those who were noticeably absent were her only brother, oldest son Joe, who refuses to attend anybody's funeral, and her youngest son Dwight, who would have probably been killed if he had come anyway.

- **Social Isolation** - I couldn't stand to be around a lot of people for quite some time, partly because I had become vulnerable to weeping when people offered their condolences and partly because I had become vulnerable to coming out of character and snapping at the simplest things. I had a reputation for being the go-to guy with an open-door policy, allowing anyone to walk into my office. Still, for months, I kept my office door closed, often sitting in the dark and seldom interacting with any of my employees.

Though the hole was never filled, as the years went by, life without a living mother became easier. The joy of being surrounded by Nicole and the children seemed to eliminate the peculiar feeling that somehow Momma had left me again, even though I felt I didn't really need her.

# The Awakening

On Christmas day of 2018, my family surprised me by purchasing a product called Ancestry, which is one of the largest genealogy websites in the world. It helps people learn about their family history and ancestry by completing the DNA kit provided. Nicole was well aware that I had a longing to know my father's relatives and had become frustrated with Daddy not sharing.

Receiving the results of my submitted DNA sample caused an awakening in me from the information given, which began to quench my thirst to know who I was. I could finally see the makeup of the blood that ran through my veins:

- *24% Nigeria*

- *21% Benin & Togo*

- *13% Cameroon*

- *12% Ivory Coast & Ghana*

- *10% Western Bantu Peoples*

- *7% Mali*

- 3% Senegal

- 3% Scotland

- 2% England & Northwestern Europe

- 1% each - Yorubaland, Central West Africa, Nigerian Woodlands, Southern Bantu Peoples, and Indigenous Americas - North

In essence, my blood is 94% African, 5% European, and 1% Indigenous North American!

I began to build my family tree using the app with the names of the people I actually knew. Then, I was mesmerized that the program not only gave hints of possible relatives based on my submissions, but also daily clues of relatives based on DNA centimorgan (cM), which is a unit of measurement used to indicate the genetic distance between two points on a chromosome. In essence, the cM essentially represents the likelihood that two genes will be inherited together due to their proximity; the higher the cM number, the more closely related two individuals are likely to be based on the amount of shared DNA they have.

Like a kid in a candy store, I would spend hours after work connecting my Wadley lineage while taking notes on the multiple people who kept popping up as relative matches with 200 to 813 cMs of people with last names of which I had never even heard. The highest cMs that I had not discarded were:

1.  Nicole Carteret - 813 cM

2.  Dorthy Gordon - 609 cM

3.  *C.P. - 522 cM

4.  Olifphia Kennedy - 514 cM

5.  Tamika Phillips - 471 cM

6.  Kellie Marks - 426 cM

7.  Amanda Gillam - 238 cM

I spent almost two years after receiving my results exploring the hints of Ancestry, staring at the unknown names from time to time while building my family tree. On March 6, 2021, I noticed that the app had a feature that allows you to send a private message through the program and decided to send the following message to Nicole Carteret, who had the highest cM match on my list:

"Good afternoon, Nicole. Ancestry just informed me you are my first cousin. My name is Des Pennington, and I'm attempting to figure out who my family is."

Before the day was over, I received this response:

"Des, this is Nikki (Nicole), your aunt. Your grandfather George's youngest daughter. OMG!!!"

I had just found my Aunt Nicole, who I had been searching for since shortly after Granddaddy passed! Our discussion upon my immediate call revealed that she had long since left Atlanta, got married, and moved to Virginia. By April, I took my family on vacation to Virginia to both hug her neck and introduce my youngest children to my mother's baby sister, Auntie Nicole Carteret! Using that service, I also sent similar messages to Olifphia, Tamika, Kellie, and Amber, among others, to see if I would have similar success. I eagerly awaited a response from any on the list because I was concerned that the only Pennington I had received a match for was C.P., who I realized was my oldest brother Joe's granddaughter, Charlie Pennington. Then, on May 13, 2021, I began communicating with Amber Gilliam, followed by Tamika Phillips on May 17, 2021, who had both responded to my messages sent on March 30th and April 8th, respectively. The three of us spent the next year building individual relationships as cousins, attempting to figure out how we were related.

## My DNA Cousins

Tamika already knew we had to be related on her father's side because though she knew him, she and her mother were estranged from that side of the family, with most finding out she existed at his funeral. She and I hit it off instantly because she actually got on Ancestry to connect with her father's relatives as well and found she had an older brother she had never met. Amanda, however, was the true catalyst in our search, keeping Tamika and me abreast of her research as she did the heavy digging. In frustration one day, as Amanda and I talked on the phone, she informed me that she was going to have her mother join Ancestry and have her take a DNA test. When her mom received her results, Amanda called me and asked me to sit down. She announced, "We don't know how, but you are more of a DNA match with my mother than with me!

Frustrated, I decided to leave the app Ancestry alone and hire a genealogist, who turned out to be simply a waste of my money, leaving me back at square one! Almost a year later, on June 11, 2022, I woke up early in the morning and decided to scroll through Ancestry, having not even so much as looked at it for a while. I was intrigued when I saw a familiar last name with a 405 cM match - Blendale Moore. I was contacted through Ancestry by a cousin in Ohio named Cynthia Moore in June 2021, who was assisting in determining our match, but our cM was only sixty-two. With a second Moore, and a much higher cM match, thoughts ran through my head that my youngest brother's father, Desmond, might actually be *my* birth father and the reason I wasn't getting any Pennington matches. Taking a deep breath, I sent Blendale the message that I communicated to all Ancestry matches. Within minutes, Blendale responded.

"Yes, I see we are related. I would like to converse with you. Perhaps we can discover the side to which we are related. I know already. If you care to reach out again thru other conduits, my contact info is xxx-xxx-xxxx."

Since it was Saturday, I decided to give Blendale a call, especially considering that she believed she already knew.

She and I spent over two hours on the phone, comparing the names showing as DNA matches from our individual accounts. Blendale would say a name, and I would simply respond, "Yes" or "No." By the end of the comparison, she asked me if I was sitting down.

*Why does everybody keep asking me if I am sitting down?* I thought.

It turned out Blendale was concerned that what she was seeing would have a negative effect on me, which was evident when she made a statement concerning being careful with what she was about to say. After assuring her that I was perfectly fine, she asked a question that has always been, in my mind. It was the elephant in the room.

"Is there any way Mr. Pennington is *not* your biological father?"

I confided in her that I had explicitly contacted her because I may be the son of my younger brother's father, Desmond Moore. Without hesitation, she definitely put that belief to bed by revealing that her last name was Moore through marriage. There was no way that our cM would be in the 400's if Desmond was my father. When Blendale told me her maiden name was Hilliard, however, it sent shockwaves down my spine. That name was the one that had been repeated over and over again as a match that I kept denying as accurate through the system. She further revealed that our common matches pointed to Edna Hilliard Davis as my paternal grandmother.

Blendale explained that she came to that conclusion after sharing Edna had three children who were her first cousins: Willie Fred Davis, Thomas Davis, and Betsy Gwendolyn Davis Miree. Then further explained that:

- Tamika Phillips (471 cM) was Thomas Davis' daughter.

- Kellie Marks (426 cM) was Gwendolyn Davis Miree's granddaughter.

- Then, to make things more coincidental, it turns out that Blendale was actually Amanda Gillam's mother, but I had no idea since Amanda had never told me her mother's name.

Through Ancestry, I may have unknowingly been talking to my paternal family for over a year and had no idea.

# Connecting the Dots

I t turned out that Willie Fred Davis left Crystal Springs, Mississippi, in 1967 and moved to Detroit to work at Ford Motor Company, bringing his younger brother Thomas later that year or in the early months of 1968. After three-way calls with Thomas, Jr. (Tamika Phillips' older brother) and Olifphia Kennedy (Blendale's sister), we concluded that either Willie Fred or Thomas was my biological father. Enda Hillard Davis, Thomas, Sr., and Betsy Gwen Davis Miree had died, and Willie Fred Davis was alive and still living in Detroit, though he suffered from diabetes. When asked how I wished to proceed, I purchased Ancestry for Thomas, Jr., who lived in Colorado, and asked that Blendale set up a meeting with Willie Fred Davis because he was the oldest living person on my paternal side. He was either my father or my uncle. To make things even more uncanny, since Blendale lived in California, she called her cousin in Detroit to assist with the introduction.

Her cousin Samantha and I already knew each other. She was a close friend and a sorority sister of my wife. Not to mention, her son Steven and I were in the same fraternity, serving the community in the same chapter.

Because Willie Fred was ill, and she had not seen him in quite some time, Samantha and Blendale asked me to wait for a while, which would give them a chance to ease this information on the family. Though I agreed, I researched the name Willie Fred Davis. It gave me an address in Detroit on a familiar street not too far from my Uncle George, where I used to live. What was more surprising is that his home was within walking distance from the church at which I was ordained.

For weeks, I was on another emotional rollercoaster. All kinds of thoughts ran through my head about who this man was and how he would respond to knowing that I was part of the family. After work, I would go out of my way and periodically drive past his house, trying to get a glimpse of its occupants. At times, I'd park two doors down to watch for movement before going home. I was in turmoil because I decided to keep my findings secret from everyone, except my wife. I spent multiple sleepless nights in expectation of knowing yet preparing myself for the rejection that more than likely would happen. Until one day, I couldn't take the mental anguish anymore. I decided I would call Daddy just to ease my mind.

When he answered the phone after short pleasantries, I asked him if he had a few minutes to talk about a personal issue with me. Upon his agreement, I built up enough courage to let him know what was going on. Instead of just coming out with what had happened, I began with, "You know I have always honored you as my father, so I want to let you know I recently did Ancestry and…"

Before I could even finish my sentence, he made a statement that crushed my very soul.

"Boobie, I've always known you were not my son! Your mother and I decided that I would sign the birth certificate. Sometimes, adults just make those decisions. Leave it alone; I signed the certificate, so I *am* your father."

I was fifty-three years old. Yet, hearing him make that statement transported me back to that little boy terrified of a man while realizing he took the frustration of a cheating wife out on her illegitimate son. The smell of poverty, the feeling of helplessness, and the sense of fear that I had long placed behind me returned from those words. Didn't he know that I struggled with looking a man in the eyes because of him and had recently grown to a place where I could confidently speak to crowds after years of abuse? He knew I was not his son when he introduced himself by beating me in front of my siblings the day he walked into my life. He knew I wasn't his son, and he and my mother chose not to tell me. With tears running down my face, before hanging up the phone, I told Joseph Pennington, "You will *never* hear from me again."

I wanted to jump on a plane and slap him unconscious, choking him until he died. I wanted my lick back! I knew that I had too much to lose, but the very remembrance of how he treated me as a boy and the constant rejection throughout my life, knowing he knew, made me want *revenge*. He didn't deserve to be in my life. Though physical violence would satisfy my need for justification, I decided that cutting him off would forever remove him from all communication with his natural kids, who only communicated with him through me. In my mind, Joseph Benjamin Pennington, Sr. died that day while I desperately returned to the place of despair of the young man in me.

After a few days, still somewhat heated, I called Uncle George to tell him what had transpired concerning what Joseph had revealed, only for him to tell me that he *always* knew, as well! He then went on to explain that he didn't feel it was his place to tell me. According to him, knowing Momma's secret was one of the reasons he chose not to have a relationship with her.

Infuriated with his logic, knowing that he had ample time to tell me the truth as well, I told him that all the adults in my life had failed me and hung up the phone. They knew I was abused and abandoned. They left me to fend for myself.

I longed to know my family, yet not one of them had the decency to tell me I wasn't a Pennington! I was enraged at Joseph Pennington, Uncle George, and my deceased mother for having me uncover her secret after her death.

# The Big Reveal

My life had been reduced to a depressed man sitting two doors down from the address I had found, afraid to get out of the car and just knock on the door. Like a little child, I sat in my car weeping, too terrified to move. Deep down, I understood my terror was due to knowing that being rejected after knocking on the door would send me into an abyss that I didn't believe I could mentally return from. Then, one day, I realized that what was happening had affected my attitude at work when I cussed out one of my junior-level employees for asking a simple question. This shocked everybody because it was out of character, as I hadn't used profanity in any setting in over twenty years! Since I was the department manager, I immediately left work for the day. I drove directly to that house and parked in the driveway! Cussing had triggered the alpha male that I had become, and on July 5, 2022, I got out of that car and knocked on the door after nobody answered the doorbell I was ringing. After about ten minutes with no answer, I wrote a note on the back of one of my business cards, dropping it into the mail slot of the screen door. It read, "My name is Des Pennington, and I'm looking for Willie Fred Davis. I'm a 53-year-old man and just found out that he may be my father."

I had finally made up my mind that there was no way I would suffer this secret alone. I now couldn't care less how my reveal affected the family behind that door. Whoever had a problem would just have to do as I had done ... and get over it!

With all my contact information on that business card, I figured I'd give them a few days to contact me before returning to their doorstep. Much to my surprise, around 5 p.m. that same day, I received a call from a woman by the name of Denese Davis, who happened to be Willie Fred's daughter. Upon her introduction and announcement that she was calling about the card I'd placed in the door, I thanked her for responding. Then I announced, "Before I begin, I need you to know I'm a financially secure family man looking for nothing but the truth."

Upon giving a brief explanation of my findings, name-dropping the family members that I had been talking to, and all that had concluded either Willie Fred or Thomas had to be my father, I concluded my dissertation with the crescendo, "DNA doesn't lie! People do!"

Denese said she would get back to me when I informed her that I would pay for his son Willie Fred, Jr. to take a

DNA test because I didn't want to disrupt her father's rest, as I knew he was sick. In my mind, if Jr's DNA returned between 700 and 800+ cMs, Willie Fred Davis, Sr. would be my birth father. If it was less than 600, Thomas Davis was the one who had a relationship with my mother. Less than an hour later, Denese called me back with shocking news. Not only had the family agreed to a DNA test, but Willie Fred, Sr. was the one who would be taking it!

Upon hearing that news, I decided that using Ancestry was not the most efficient form of testing to determine our relationship upon consulting with one of my good friends, Judge Kenneth King. While I was discussing DNA sites with Denese so we could set an appointment, letting her know I would be paying for everything, my wife came into the room excited because she had found a mobile DNA unit. Choosing that option, we set a date for the unit to come to Davis' home, where I would meet them to take the test. The date was set for Thursday, July 7, 2022.

# The DNA Test

M y wife had to drive me to the Davis home, as well as hold my hand as we walked to the door because I was extremely nervous, and my stomach was in knots. We were both totally confused and thought we were at the wrong house because the person who answered the door was a man named Jose Black, who had been in both of our lives for over twenty years. Apparently, during our two-day wait, the Davis family had gone on my Facebook page to get a glimpse of who I was. They noticed multiple pictures of Jose and me from community service events we had done together. It turns out Jose was a nephew because he was married to the niece of Willie Fred's wife, Jettie Miree Davis, whom everybody called Momma Bay.

With a big grin that instantly eased my nerves, Jose welcomed us into a house filled with the most hospitable people I had ever met in my life! They were all grinning from ear to ear as I introduced myself. They stared at me with mouths wide open as though they had seen a ghost after my introduction. When I reached the chair where Willie Fred sat, I could see why they looked at me like that.

Looking at him was as though I was looking into my own face, but as an older man! As I glanced over his shoulder, I almost burst into tears after I saw a picture on his mantle of him as a young boy who looked *exactly* like my son Joshua! While waiting for the unit to arrive, Momma Bay ordered her girls to set up a family dinner and she made sure we were fed.

As the mobile unit personnel administered the test, I could hear rumblings in the room as photos were being taken. It was evident that they had no doubt I was family. Even after the testing was complete and taken away for diagnostics, the family told me stories of the Hilliards and Mirees, who just so happened to be Momma Bay's maiden name. As I learned that a Davis brother and sister, Willie Fred and Betsy Gwen, had married a Miree sister and brother, Jettie and Theodore, making some of the family "double cousins," Momma Bay passed around family photo albums displaying the years of family reunions. I was further elated while looking through the albums when I saw Craig Miree, Jr. and his lovely wife Brandi, along with his parents and sisters. I had known them for over ten years as members of a church I was once one of the assistant pastors. What was even more uncanny was that Brandi Miree was considered to be Nicole and my oldest daughter because we let her live with us before she got married while she was in college.

Whether Willie Fred, Sr. was my father or my uncle, I found out that I had been surrounded by my father's people for a significant portion of my life and had developed decade-long relationships, not knowing we were blood relatives. Before leaving, the Davis' invited me to come back to their home on Sunday, July 17 to help them celebrate Willie Fred's birthday. Unfortunately, I had to decline the offer because I was taking my family on vacation, and our flight left that Sunday morning. Later that week, I received a call informing me that they had changed the party to Saturday, July 16 to make sure I could attend. We hadn't even received the results from the DNA test, and these people changed the party date so I could attend! *Who does that?!*

On July 13, I received a call about the results of our DNA test. With 99.97%, Willie Fred Davis, Sr. was proven to be my biological father! When I called Momma Bay and Denese with tears rolling down my face to give them the news— I could hear screeches of elation coming from the people in the Davis household because, according to Momma Bay, they didn't need a blood test as soon as they laid eyes on me. My sister Denese yelled in the background, "I knew it ... y'all even laugh the same!" Momma Bay let me know that she wasn't gonna tell my daddy but instead wanted me to give him the news at his birthday party.

Though Daddy was a double amputee and blind due to complications from his diabetes, his mind was still sharp. As his family and friends gathered in his backyard for the barbecue in his honor, showering him with his birthday presents, he would say their names after they greeted him and thank them for their gifts. When it was my turn, I let him know I was the young man who had taken a DNA test with him and that I wanted to give him two gifts.

- I first presented him with silk pajamas because I noticed from the photos he enjoyed the finer things in life.

- Then I explained that I was giving him a copy of a 5 X 7 framed photo created from one of the pictures taken of him and me after the test that had a special message in the back of it.

Taking his copy of the DNA testing out of the frame, I read him the results. We both openly wept because I had found my father, and he had found his son! With not a dry eye in his backyard, Daddy composed himself and declared with all his strength, "My son, I apologize for not being in your life before, but I promise you from this day forward, as long as I have breath in my body, I'll be there!"

One of my proudest moments was the day he showed up with his entire household to hear me preach the Gospel at my church. I cried when he called me to let me know how gifted I was and that he was proud to be my father. Daddy and I spent time together at a minimum once a week, building a relationship, never forgetting to say, "I love you" to one another before I left him. During one of my visits, I decided to ask him if he remembered a lady by the name of Loretta Pennington, even though it really didn't matter if he remembered Momma because it was so long ago. Daddy raised his head as though he were looking into the sky and shared that all he remembered was that they were together until one day, she just dropped off the face of the earth. As I contemplated what he had said, I remember thinking, *If you could see me, you'd be looking at the face!*

It turns out that Daddy and Momma met sometime after he arrived in Detroit, and they hit it off pretty well, though he never asked if he knew she was married or not. According to him, Momma would hang out from time to time until, one day, she just stopped coming around. With our recent revelation, we can only reach the conclusion that Momma found out she was pregnant with me, went back to her husband, and ended the affair. They decided to never tell my father about his baby. My father met and married Jettie Miree a year after I was born and raised her two daughters, not knowing I existed while praying that he would have a son one day. The Davises were a blended family of five girls because he had three daughters of his own from his first marriage. He and Momma Bay were elated when they found out that she was having a boy after eleven years of marriage, whom they proudly named Willie Fred Davis, Jr.

In addition to raising their own children, the Davises housed many family members throughout the years, helping until they got back on their feet. Hearing the recants of the past made me understand myself more and more each day, as many of the stories were actually things that Nicole and I had done throughout our marriage. My newly found family loved me with the love that I had longed for. I wanted them to know how much I appreciated it so much that I convinced my older sisters Debra, who resided in Atlanta, and Gloria in Crystal Springs, to meet Denese, Fred, Jr., and me in Detroit for Thanksgiving. I wanted Daddy to have all of his natural children in the same house for the first time. Our father was shocked when we all showed up and had his photo taken with all five of his children. My wife created refrigerator magnets for each of us and gave them to each of us as Christmas gifts.

Unfortunately, on March 14, 2023, at the age of eighty-three, my father, Willie Fred Davis, Sr., passed away. Though I lost my father nine months after we found out about each other, it was the most rewarding nine months of my life. I was there with my paternal family as the coroner retrieved Daddy's remains for transport to the funeral home. Daddy left this world to cherish his memory: a devoted wife of fifty-three years, six children (one preceded him in death), ten grandchildren, and three great-grandchildren.

Sitting between my older sisters at our father's funeral, I realized that life is a marathon. It's essential to take the time necessary to allow all the pieces of the puzzle to fall into place. I may have started my race by tripping at the gate, but my recovery has been simply remarkable! Since I understand that we run the race of life through seasons, I will spend this next season living, loving, and learning about my family.

Without a shadow of a doubt, today I can confidently say that my name is Des Arnel Davis, although the last name on my birth certificate says Pennington because Momma wanted it that way. Finally, I know who I am and whose I am!

# About the Author

While many spend a lifetime struggling to define their identity, he learned that his was tucked away in his most challenging times. As an agent of change, pastor, community leader and humanitarian, Des A. Pennington is best known for his unique perspective on life delivered through poetry, storytelling, preaching and speaking. Understanding that our personal tests are both for our growth, as well as the growth and edification of others, Des specializes in helping people worldwide discover their purpose, find fulfillment and connect the dots in life when nothing makes sense.

As a United States Marine and a veteran of the Persian Gulf War, Des spent more than 26 years in leadership in corporate America. In addition to several professional awards and accolades, he has been fortunate to serve for years with Phi Beta Sigma Fraternity, Inc., 100 Black Men of Greater Detroit and the Board of Directors for The Croghan Foundation. Des has constantly ranked in the top 1% of members in his fraternity in fundraising efforts—no matter the endeavor. He has also personally donated thousands of dollars toward scholarships for deserving children on their way to college.

A servant leader at heart, Des faithfully served in various pastoral roles for more than 30 years in five different ministries. Today, he is the Director of Pastoral Care at Impact Church of Detroit. He strives diligently and daily to live Revelation 12:11 (KJV): *And they overcame him by the blood of the Lamb, and by the word of their testimony; and they loved not their lives unto the death.* In his debut book, *Rejected: The Story of an African American Man in Search of Himself,* he takes readers on an authentic journey of healing, hope and direction for men of all ages who are struggling to find their true identity. From abuse and poverty to rejection and redemption, this candid literary masterpiece empowers readers to go from victim to victor.

Devoted husband to Nicole and father of three (Destiny, Joshua and Lauryn), Des and his wife have raised more than twenty-three children. Through becoming foster parents before having children of their own, they allowed mothers with small children to live in their home for up to a year to save money. At the core of their being, they genuinely believe it's the community's responsibility to care for the needy. So, they're always the first to spring into action.

For booking or speaking engagements, email
despenningtonbooking@gmail.com or call 313.444.5216.

www.ingramcontent.com/pod-product-compliance
Lightning Source LLC
Chambersburg PA
CBHW071750120626
46550CB00002B/738